Queer Astrology for Men

ALSO BY JILL DEARMAN

Queer Astrology for Women: An Astrological Guide for Lesbians

Queer Astrology for Men

An Astrological Guide for Gay Men

Jill Dearman

St. Martin's Griffin
New York

BOOK DESIGN: JAMES SINCLAIR

ILLUSTRATIONS: MARK NESTON

Library of Congress Cataloging-in-Publication Data

Dearman, Jill.
    Queer astrology for men: an astrological guide for gay men / by Jill Dearman.
       p.   cm.
    ISBN 0-312-19952-X
    1. Astrology and homosexuality.   2. Gay men—Miscellanea. 3. Love—Miscellanea.   I. Title.
BF1729.H66D43   1999
133.5'83067662—dc21   98-37646
                                          CIP

First St. Martin's Griffin Edition: February 1999

10 9 8 7 6 5 4 3 2 1

Dedication

Many people have helped to elevate me to the humble status I now enjoy as "Astrologer to the Stars." I dedicate this book to my lover, **Andrea Kleine,** for all her love, support, and passion. I would also like to thank **James Cassese** for being my contract angel and a force of brotherly Aquarian love, **Penny Perkins** for her generosity in sharing the secrets of her famous address book, **Charlie Spicer** for fabulous editing and all the kind, smart folks at St. Martin's Press, **Ralph Vicinanza,** my agent, for rich astrological understanding and for hooking me up with St. Martin's Press, **Matthew Bank and the HX staff** for giving me a forum in NYC's gay community, **Deborah Taylor** for giving me my first byline as an astrologer back in college, **Maria Napoli** for being the greatest astrologer who's ever lived, **Brian McCormack** for being a best friend and a brilliant muse, and **my family** for their love and support of my astrological sleuthing.

I would also like to thank my pals **Allan, Hope, Wagner, Maureen, Clarinda, Philip, Aydin, Alice, Suz, Wendy Jo, Chris, Karen, Maura,** and **Rachel,** who have always encouraged me to do something a little bit different from the pack and who have indulged me in mock-guru status when my moon in Aries needed a boost.

And special thanks to all the darling folks who have read my astrology columns, come to see me as private clients, and given me generous feedback over the years. I hope this book gives you as much insight as you've given me. All I ever wanted was to amuse and enlighten you great individuals and the magnificent masses!

Contents

Introduction

How can a woman write for gay men? you may ask. Well, some women are gay men on the inside, like me. I'm not a show tune fan, but I love what you boys do with leather, circuit parties, and track lighting. I've always been a fan of the way you fellows lead your lives: using sex as a weapon (as Pat Benatar would say), and adding creativity to whatever project you pursue. Call me a starstruck stargazer, but it's true, dammit, all true. All right, maybe you can see through my flattery, but you boys have responded with immense praise for the gay-male astrology columns I've written over the years, and this book is my way of saying, "Right back at you, boys."

Now let's talk astrology.

Boys. Boys. Boys. Where do we begin? This book is intended to be an "Astrology 101" course for gay men (and the folks like me who love you). And so we will begin with the basics: the twelve Sun signs. Keep in mind, my darlings, that your Sun sign is only one small part of your chart. No two Virgos are alike, for example, (although I defy you to find me one Virgo who is not prone toward the obsessive!), but people born under the same Sun sign do share many similarities. Think of the signs as archetypes, like the Gods and Goddesses of ancient mythology.

If you have your natal chart, you may want to read up on your moon sign, which rules your emotional nature, and your rising sign (also called the ascendant), which will tell you about your appearance and how other people perceive you. You may even want to look up the sign your Venus is in to see what kind of lover you are. By doing this you will get into the hang of balancing the different parts of an individual chart.

In later books, I hope to teach you all how to understand the more intricate parts of your chart (and the charts of your lovers, family, and friends) . . . from aspects between the planets to transits and retrogrades and past lives. But in this book, we'll stick to the basics.

An important thing to remember when reading this book is that all the signs are divided into four elements (fire, earth, air, and water) and three modes (cardinal, fixed, and mutable).

The fire signs (Aries, Leo, and Sagittarius) are known for being action-oriented, direct and honest, and a little bit naive. Fire signs are ruled by passion and their own egos. They are great at parties but sometimes get antsy when the fun is over. The earth signs (Taurus, Virgo, and Capricorn) are practical and enjoy the simple things in life. These boys all pray to the goddess of work and appreciate the things that money can buy. The earth-sign boys are slaves to their bodies (whether they obsess about their health or just need a lot more hugging and touching than the next man). The air signs (Gemini, Libra, and Aquarius) are cerebral. They are ruled by their minds and live most happily in the world of ideas. Life with an air sign is bound to be . . . well . . . rather *chatty*. They can talk their way into or out of anything, but sometimes get confused when the subject is their own feelings. The water signs (Cancer, Scorpio, and Pisces) are slaves to their emotions. These guys feel first and think later. They are intuitive, mysterious, and *moody* as hell! Their feelings are deep and they live for love, but can sometimes nurse a broken heart or lick an old wound for years.

Now let's look at the modes of the signs, which will show you how each sign of each element is different from her sisters. First are the cardinal signs (Aries, Cancer, Libra, and Capricorn). These guys are the leaders of the zodiac. They have the initiative and organizational skills to get projects (and relationships!) under way. Aries has the energy to start things. Cancer can pull people together in a gentle, personal way. Libras have a clear vision of what the finished product should be. And Capricorns see the bottom line.

The second group are the fixed signs (Taurus, Leo, Scorpio, and Aquarius). These fellows have the staying power to *finish* what's been started. They are tenacious and patient, but stubborn, stubborn, stubborn. These guys are not known for their flexibility. But they are known for their reliability. Taurus knows how to stay the course. Leo is known for his loyalty and dedication. Scorpio never gives up. And Aquarius wants to see change occur, no matter how long it takes.

The last group are the mutable signs (Gemini, Virgo, Sagittarius, and Pisces). These gay boys are known for being adaptable. They are survivors who can adjust to any situation and environment because of their flexibility. Each one is a chameleon in his own way. As a group, though, they can be a little vague! Geminis jump from idea to idea, learning more with each one. Virgos aren't snobbish about the work they do. They thrive on the details—whether it's cleaning the oven or fact-checking the encyclopedia. Sagittarius is always looking for a new religion. He is an adventurer constantly testing his own philosophies. And Pisces is an emotional cushion. He absorbs all the feelings around him.

I hope this book helps you to understand yourself and the important men in your life a little bit better. For me, the more I write about astrology, the more questions I am left with. I wish you luck on your journey and hope you learn something valuable from the following chapters.

Finally, if you view this book as pure entertainment, fine. Just leave the money on the dresser. If your interest in astrology runs deeper, I encourage you to learn more, whenever you are ready. And remember, sweeties: In astrology, timing is *everything*.

One

The Twelve Sun Signs

♈ ♉ ♊ ♋ ♌ ♍ ♎ ♏ ♐ ♑ ♒ ♓

Aries

(March 21—April 20)

Element: Fire
Mode: Cardinal
Ruling Planet: Mars
Erogenous Zone: Head, face
Best Traits: Brave, thoroughly unjaded, energetic
Worst Traits: Oblivious, dominating (see *caveman*), dangerously impulsive

♈ ♉ ♊ ♋ ♌ ♍ ♎ ♏ ♐ ♑ ♒ ♓

In Life

The Aries gay man is a primal force. He is strong and butch, even when he's wearing a skirt, and rarely has an indecisive moment. Even the softer ones are real "daddies" on the inside. He must feel like the master of his own destiny at all times and cannot even bear to admit to himself if he feels clueless. It's not that he's a control queen (see Capricorn for that), it's just that the darling boy loves to be in charge. He needs to be his own boss first, and then he can boss you around. And he will, honey.

Mr. Aries could be any of the members of the Village People . . . the cop, the cowboy, the construction worker. He loves to play roles, and the more obvious the better. Subtlety is not exactly one of his strong points . . . in fact, come to think of it, he possesses none! What he does have a lot of is heart and honesty. He really hates to lie and does it so poorly that he knows it's not even worth the effort.

Although on occasion he may tell you how beautiful that cockring looks with that string of faux pearls, just to make you happy and to get you on your back that much faster.

And speaking of faster, pussycat, this man is a veritable speed machine. He goes through life at 150 miles an hour, and he is just as fast and furious in bed. (So that the fast part doesn't frustrate you, *you* had better get in charge of the foreplay department.)

On the outside, Mr. Aries may seem egotistical and vain, and certainly self-centered, but, you know, he is really a lot more than that. If we were all as up-front about what we want and how we feel, there would be a lot less war and misery in the world and a lot less cattiness in our own little gay ghetto. So take a lesson from him. He is who he is and does not pretend to be anyone else. He 'fesses up to his own shit, and that's what makes him braver than most. He also has high expectations of himself, and if he doesn't let you into his psyche that easily, it might be because he is still trying to prove himself *to* himself. He may have a big ego, but he is by no means smug.

This man is a true innocent in the world and wants to make his own way on his own terms, without having to lie, cheat, or steal to get to the top. But get to the top he will, because he is a true individual and a real risk-taker, in the best possible sense. He's a rare breed, and he knows it.

In Bed

He's an animal, I tell you, an animal! Mr. Aries loves to conquer, even if he's the one getting tied up and fisted. He brings a beastlike kind of passion to all sexual encounters, and that rough-and-ready MO will not wane as time passes. Some people just crackle with sexual energy and he's one of them.

He can be just a tad one-note, though. Mr. Aries is good in the beginning (grabbing you roughly and kissing as if he means it), and good in the end (coming like a wild man and pushing you to do the same), but in the middle you may have to train him to please you. As I mentioned, he's not exactly a prince of subtlety, so the little details that bring you great pleasure could elude him. So if you just love to have your bare butt spanked before being entered (and who doesn't?), or if you like to have your feet rubbed and licked before you get down to anything heavier, then I suggest you let him know, and let him know clearly. That means with words or with force.

And then once he gets into the habit, he may give you the same kind of loving every time, so then you'd better teach him new tricks, and then new ones after that. But unless you want him to start tricking with someone else, please make sure that you treat his fragile ego like the tender, beautiful thing it is. Make him feel good, and let him know how much he turns you on. You can never go too over the top when it comes to showing him how wild with lust he makes you.

He tends toward rough sex more than most (and since this book is for gay men, you know he must be quite a savage sister). He could care less if the room smells like patchouli incense or if your sister-in-law is doing her nails in the next room. He wants what he wants when he wants it, and spontaneity is definitely one of his strong points. He is drawn toward the dirty and likes to feel and smell as if he's just had sex with a man when the deed is done. He also likes it if you are *not* in the mood. He does find love a challenge after all. Protest too much and you will surely be screaming with ecstasy within the hour.

And remember, his head is his erogenous zone, so give that thick skull the attention it deserves, and that its owner desires. And speaking of giving, let's get real for a moment, shall we? This man honestly prefers for you to give to him, more than he needs to give to you. You know what I'm saying, girl: give him a blow job, give him your cock, or give him your ass to fuck. It's all about him darling, and if you are lusting after an Aries, I suspect that that's part of the turn-on.

How to Seduce Him

In his fantasy world, he is the man who gets what he wants. He's the gay James Bond, in a Tarzan outfit. Let him chase you down, if you really want him. Play the waiting game, because he is definitely the kind of guy who appreciates (and gets off on) a challenge.

As the mother of an Aries friend of mine once said, "The boy won't buy the cow if he can get the milk for free." Translating this into modern gay terminology: your Aries man will work a lot harder and come to you a lot faster if you don't make things too easy for him. Be a little straight-girl cock-tease, who knows she can't open her legs for every Dick, Dick, and Dick. Drive him crazy with self-restraint and let him know why you are holding back your love (the contrived reason, of course, darling, not the real one!). Tell him that you are at a point in your life where you need to move slowly and cautiously before jumping into a hot sexual tryst. Well, maybe that is the truth, but he doesn't have to know the whole truth . . . like the fact that right up until you met him, you were a complete and total slut.

Doing Him and Dating Him

The early stages of a relationship with an Aries are truly the most fun. He loves to woo and is quite irresistible when he turns on that potent physical charm. He likes to go out a lot. Dining he can take or leave, but dancing is usually an important part of the ritual. Try not to laugh at him when he shows off on the dance floor. He may have the annoying habit of "dancing with himself," but that's where you can teach him a few things, you passive whore you. A little dirty dancing goes a long way.

You will also find that he is well liked but basically marches to his own drummer. Hang out in a group . . . he will appreciate the social contact, but make no mistake, he wants to be with you and you alone, you little love object you. So, just when he seems totally "over" the communal experience, pull him off to a private corner and rub your nose against that thick brow of his. (If it's a uni-brow, all the better.) But just give him a nice long taste. Then let him decide what comes next. Remember who's the boss, honey.

How to Last over the Long Haul

Mr. Aries is at his best in the beginning of a relationship. He loves all things new and shiny, like your hot rod, sweetie. But once he has conquered you (in his own mind) or feels that he knows all there is to know about *you* in life and in bed, he will see no reason to stick around. Security is not a motivating force in his life (that's a Taurus *thang*, darling). So if you want a lasting relationship with this passionate but sometimes immature man, here's what you need to do.

Keep changing your act. If he's already seen a lot of your adventurous and athletic side, why not show him the quietly mystical part of your personality. Leave your candelabra out one night, next to your runes and tarot cards, and force him to ask you if you are a witch (he is so childlike that way!). Help him to discover the many facets of you, sweetie. He may be a one-trick pony, at times, but you don't have to be. In fact, if you show him how multilayered you are, he will be inspired to dig deeper into his bag of tricks to show you how deep and fascinating he is. He is fiercely competitive after all (but in a most refreshingly open and healthy way . . . honestly) and will not be outdone by you in the "Who's the real prize?" category. He wants you to keep reinventing yourself so that he can dig into your well of depth for inspiration, and he wants you to encourage him to be even more brave and bold and powerful than he already is. It's all about challenges, sweetie. Challenge yourself, and prod him to challenge himself, and don't be afraid to challenge each other. This man will stick around forever if he finds a partner who is as tough and courageous as he is (or as he aspires to be). If you thought the beginning of your liaison was exciting, you will experience even more thrills years down the road, if you are willing to grow a little bit. Each phase of your evolving relationship can be like a new beginning: sexy, rocky at times, but basically good, honest, and loving.

How to Get Rid of Him

So it was a fun ride while it lasted but now you're ready to say adios to your hot but unevolved Aries lover? Well, how shall we do this? He's blunt, so you might as well be. Mr. Aries would rather be let down like a ton of bricks and know how you honestly feel than to be lead on and pushed away gently. He is a force of nature, and like the disco anthem that he is sure to play twenty-four/seven after you dump him . . . he *will* survive!

But if *you* are too weak-willed to do the dirty deed in the above manner, try this for plan B: get him to do the dumping first. How, Jill darling, how, you ask? You can take two separate but equally effective approaches. You can challenge every single thing he says. Mr. Aries likes to rule the roost and run his own affairs, like a man, a real man, baby. And real men don't like to be told what to do. Start questioning all his choices, and acting like his mother, not his lover. Boss *him* around for a change. And I don't mean once in a while as a kind of foreplay. I mean constantly. He won't be able to take it. He'll crack and run out with nothing but the clothes on his back and never look behind him. And you can go back to your quiet, orderly little world, with no Aries around to make lots of noise and state the obvious regularly.

If being bossy is not your style, be *boring*. He needs a high dose of excitement in his daily life, and if you don't give him enough, he will find it elsewhere. And he won't even leave you a "Dear John" . . . I'm sorry . . ."Dear Mary" letter before he goes.

The Three Faces of Aries

Every sign is broken up into three decanates, each of which gives the Sun sign a distinctive flavor. Keep in mind, though, that the Sun enters and leaves each sign a day later or earlier during different years. Make the proper adjustments for boys born on the cusp of their sign. Wipe that dumb look off your face and just do it. All right, you Aries boys, no whining, just check an ephemeris and see what the exact dates of your (or your pal's) Sun sign were for the year in question, divide by three, and there you will find the correct decanates.

First-Decanate Aries (March 21–31): The Mars Decanate

First-decanate Aries men are known as the most Aries of all Aries. Born in the early part of the Sun's transit through the sign of the ram, these guys possess an extra dose of courage *and* naïveté. He's the most focused of the three types of Aries and is also the most like a lone wolf. He likes sex and passion but can live without a committed relationship, unless he has some especially romantic aspects in his chart. He is a true original, this guy, and is more serious than his other Aries brothers.

Second-Decanate Aries (April 1–10): The Solar Decanate

These guys need the most attention of the three types of Aries. They are the most likely to want stable relationships in their life, mainly because they know how to give freely, and are such attention whores, that they simply must ensure an audience at all times. Men born during the middle of the Aries season are a little more cautious than other Aries guys, and a little girlier, too. They like gold lamé and frills. (I don't care how conservative or manly he seems on the outside, check that locked trunk at the foot of his bed. What do you mean, how? Ask a Scorpio if you want to know how to uncover someone's secrets!) He's the most family-oriented and the most conventional of all the Aries groups.

Third-Decanate Aries (April 11–20): The Jupiter Decanate

These are the most outrageous of all Aries guys. The Sagittarius influence makes them a little bit more like high rollers in Vegas, and a little bit less focused and driven than the others. They are truly the most fun, but also the least directed of all Aries fellas. If you are looking to settle down with one of these gadabouts, you may have to wait until he has grown up a bit. They develop more seasoned philosophies of life as they grow older. The young ones need to experience lots of travel and adventure before they can turn from boyz 2 men.

If You Have His Chart

Here are some clues, if you happen to know more about him than his date of birth. If he has a healthy sampling of Libra or Taurus in his chart, he is apt to be more romantic and more relationship-oriented than the average Aries. Both those signs are ruled by Venus—the yin to his Mars-ruled yang. A busy seventh house would indicate the same thing.

If his moon is in a water sign (Cancer or particularly Scorpio or Pisces), he does probably possess more emotional range and subtlety than the average ram. Lots of mutable signs in his chart (Gemini, Virgo, Sagittarius, and Pisces) will make your Aries more flexible than the others. What are you waiting for? Get his chart done now!

♈ ♉ ♊ ♋ ♌ ♍ ♎ ♏ ♐ ♑ ♒ ♓

Taurus

(April 21–May 20)

Element: Earth
Mode: Fixed
Ruling Planet: Venus
Erogenous Zone: Neck
Best Traits: Sensual, strong, and steady
Worst Traits: Stubborn, stupid, and a slave to the TV

♈ ♉ ♊ ♋ ♌ ♍ ♎ ♏ ♐ ♑ ♒ ♓

In Life

The Taurus gay man is a powerful force to reckon with. He is ruled by loving and gentle Venus and probably has a mellow, quiet manner. You may recognize him by his slow, sexy voice. Almost all of these men are closet singers or musicians (the more confident ones share their talents with the world). Mr. Taurus is artistic, sexy, and obsessed with security. This man simply must have some money tucked away in the bank (or in his lingerie drawer) in order to feel at peace with himself and the world.

He is an earth sign after all, so he can't help but realize on the most primal level that we are living in a material world, and he is a material girl. Most of these boys do have good jobs, or at least possess the ability to make a lot of dough if they want to. They can be lazy though. The most typical Taurus gay man works superhard to make lots of money so that he can later achieve the freedom and time to do absolutely nothing. *Later* may mean different things to different Tauruses. Your Taurus may come home at night and watch TV as if it were a religious calling. Or he may go out and enjoy the sensual delights the world has to offer . . . good food, good sex . . . always keeping in mind his dream to one day be able to sit on his butt and not have to answer to anybody.

Although he possesses incredibly refined tastes (I could write a whole chapter on his taste buds), at heart he has simple *needs*. Unlike his Leo brothers who really desire the good life or his Gemini brothers who need constant entertainment, Mr. Taurus can do just fine with a simple meal (which includes potatoes—his mother's milk substitute) and a bed with either a good book on his pillow or a remote control. He is self-sufficient and can take care of himself without bothering anybody. Once he is in a place in life (emotionally and practically) to do what he really wants to do, he will probably be happiest working in a field that brings his artistic talents and his smart business sense together. And then he can really feel free to enjoy himself, and all the treats the world has to offer.

In Bed

Mr. Taurus comes to life slowly but deliciously when he is making love. Although, when they have to (or feel they have to), these boys can just fuck fast and hard and go home, that's not what they're all about. Every spot on this man's body is sensitive to the touch, no matter how rough or unresponsive he may at first appear. He has to be a little tough to protect himself from his own desires. Most Tauruses, however, are affectionate. They feel they can express so much more through touching, rather than through communicating with words. That's why some Taurus guys have a bit of a prehistoric edge to them. Just think of him as the Java man ('cause he also digs a perfect cup of coffee the morning after).

You can gauge how well things are going by how much time he takes in bed. If he is feeling untrusting, or just not into it, it will be over before you can say, "Oh, baby, that feels so . . ." If he's into it, he will spend lots of time exploring the luxury of your body from head to toe, and he will growl his pleasure at your touch. When he is feeling aroused, you will find yourself getting more and turned on by how responsive he is to your every touch. Although he likes the occasional quick, dirty bang, what he really lives for is prolonged, sensual ecstasy. His attitude is "What's the rush?"

On the kinkier, or rather the messier, side, you can probably get him going by bringing his favorite foods into your sexual escapades. Let him make a meal out of you using his favorite flavors from hot strawberry syrup to chocolate espresso beans. (You said you'd play, now let him put them wherever he wants.)

And when you are *doin'* him, take your time. He can lie back and enjoy it for a long, long time. And you'll find that the older he is (or gets), the more he enjoys really playing daddy, which means sitting there with his cigar, in his slippers, and receiving your endless adoration, *sonny boy.*

How to Seduce Him

The Taurus will only allow himself to be seduced if he really wants to be. So if you are getting some response from him already, consider that a good sign. This man will not budge in a direction that he does not feel comfortable moving in. He is likely to give you subtle and yet obvious signals if he's interested. You know the kind of person who stares just a little too much and snuggles up just a little too close on the couch next to you, or who keeps touching you as he talks? That's Taurus.

If you are ready to take one on, here's some practical advice on snaring this very practical man.

Find out his routine, and learn it. This man's schedule is predictable as clockwork, even if he has three jobs and an ex-wife (in name only of course) to support. Realistically, though, most Tauruses try to keep their routines relatively simple, because they like life to be simple, and they hate to rush. So don't you dare pull any big surprises on him. If you call him on a Saturday morning and say, "Forget your soccer game. I have two tickets to a matinee of *Death of a Salesman* in drag!" you will have turned him off for good. Spontaneity annoys him. He likes to plan, and so should you.

Here's what to do: get involved in his routine. If he goes to the same sleazy dive for a cocktail at 7 P.M. every Thursday, then for goodness' sake, be there, my friend! Scope him out, and make your-self a visual fixture in his psyche. He's an easygoing person, so chances are he'll speak to you first, but if not, strike up a casual conversation with him during your third Thursday out.

Once you've got his attention, do something traditional, classy, and datelike. You boys aren't lesbians so you should both *know* that you're on a date. Go out for a luxurious dinner. He adores good food, and to him food truly is an aphrodisiac. Go to a concert or a show. He likes the simple, good things in life, and you had better like them, too, because the man has excellent taste, and although he rides the extremes of stinginess and generosity, he better not sense that you like to scrimp on what's important.

Give him the gift of music. Make him a tape; it could be the first music you get it on to, so make it smooth and sexy, baby.

Doing Him and Dating Him

The early stages of your relationship with a Taurus man are likely to be sweet and sexy. As I mentioned, he lives by his routines and dies by them, so once you are part of his world, you will experience the honor of becoming part of the structure and fabric of his daily life. Mr. Taurus is reliable, and unlike most unchivalrous and tacky whores, these days, when he says he is going to call, he will call you. You will probably find this kind of consistency and maturity quite refreshing and endearing, and even if you don't (say, if you have every planet in Sag and love to be wild and crazy all the time), I bet his gallant style will grow on you.

Sexually, you will find that this man creeps up on you like the heat from a fireplace on a cold winter's night. Once he feels com-fortable enough with you, he can be surprisingly creative and ex-perimental. He will enjoying discovering your body limb by limb, touch by touch, and at that point you should consider yourself a lucky lad.

Quality of life is superimportant to him, even if he's in the "poor student" phase of his life. He will still give you a better-quality towel to dry yourself with after a shower at his pad than you will find in your own home, or your cheap mother's. The man has got the right touch.

How to Last over the Long Haul

Taurus men love to be in relationships, and they get attached and stay attached more easily than most of those cads out there. Let's face it, he's more of a "dog person" than a "cat person" (figuratively and probably literally) when it comes to relationships. The more he sees you in his day-to-day life, the more he *wants* to see you.

The main drawback of life with a Taurus is this: he can get so set in his ways that you may find yourself bored out of your bloody mind. And unless you are out of love with him and have already skipped to "How to Get Rid of Him," you may not even realize it. He is so strong and has such a quiet but irresistible influence on your life, that you may get sucked into the death knell of his lifestyle, which might go something like this: eat, work, sleep, and occasionally fuck, unless he feels his puppy or his car hasn't been getting enough attention, in which case it may get priority over you.

It is up to you, O lover of the Taurus man, to exert your influence tenderly but firmly on your stick-in-the-mud, bull boyfriend. Every season, develop new routines and rituals that you can both share in. Once you gently and patiently work on him, this boy may end up in love with the ski slopes and more in love with you, even if he claims to "hate" winter sports. And he will have you to thank for this new and added dimension of quality in his life. He can be a handful, and he is stubborn, but you should never forget that you've got yourself a good, good man (even when you feel like wrapping his beloved potato chip bag around his head and suffocating him).

How to Get Rid of Him

Breaking up with a Taurus is not easy. First of all, even if you feel trapped and oppressed by him, he has probably become such a fixture in your life that you may find it heartbreaking to leave the big lug. And realistically, it's probably *his* apartment, *his* friends, and *his* way of life that you are going to say good-bye to, and you may just miss that stuff along with the dear and demanding Bull himself.

But if your mind is made up, then you've got your work cut out for you. Here's the sneaky and immature method first (oh, I know you would *never* stoop to it, but . . .).

Become wildly erratic. Come home at all hours, move his furniture around. Cook for him. And cook all the things he hates. If you can find new things to cook for him that he has never eaten before but that you are sure he will despise, I can virtually guarantee that he will dump you like a hot potato . . . oh, I forgot, he loves potatoes . . . well, you know what I mean, darling.

If you've been involved with your Taurus man for a while and really don't want to hurt him horribly, here's the compassionate approach.

First, be honest. He's strong and he can take it, even if breaking up is not what he wants. Honestly, these boys are meant to be in relationships, so I can tell you now . . . don't cry too many tears for him . . . he will replace you with a new and improved model within the year. So after you've dropped the bomb on him, try to develop new, transitional routines to take you both through that awkward stage, after you are "over" but before your new and separate lives have begun. If he's used to seeing you every day, wean him off you. See him for dinner once a week for a while. And stay consistent. That means same time, same night of the week, same place.

And when it's all finally over, make sure it's amicable, because I guarantee you will be knocking on his door someday in the future to borrow money.

The Three Faces of Taurus

Every sign is broken up into three decanates, each of which gives the Sun sign a distinctive flavor. Keep in mind, though, that the Sun enters and leaves each sign a day later or earlier during different years. Make the proper adjustments for boys born on the cusp of their sign. Wipe that dumb look off your face and just do it. All right, you Tauruses, no whining, just check an ephemeris and see what the exact dates of your (or your pal's) Sun sign were for the year in question, divide by three, and there you will find the correct decanates.

First-Decanate Taurus (April 21–30): The Venus Decanate

He's the most bullish of the Bulls, baby. First-decanate Tauruses possess the most potent Taurus traits, the good and the bad. These boys are the most likely to have musical gifts, and they tend to be great cooks, too. They are incredibly sensitive to their environment and the most resistant to change. Oy, is he stubborn! He may take the longest figuring out what his life calling is, but once he does, he will stick with it for the rest of his life. Hopefully, the vocation he pursues will require that he use his tremendous creative gifts.

As a lover, this "early" Taurus will be passionate but immovable. Getting him to try new things is difficult, but worth your while. He is resistant to change, and any form of abruptness rattles him. He's tough on the outside, but tremendously sensitive on the inside. I bet you've never heard that before!

Second-Decanate Taurus (May 1–10): The Mercury Decanate

These "middle" Tauruses are more flexible than the others. They are influenced by the mutable (adaptable, flexible) and service-oriented sign of Virgo. Second-decanate Tauruses are more *process*-oriented than the other Tauruses, who are more concerned with the bottom line. These Taurus gay men love to work with their hands. Most of them are great gardeners with super green thumbs. And they will find plenty to do with the rest of their fingers, too.

In bed these Tauruses like to give more than the others, which is certainly a good thing. But, they can also be the most clinical. He may like to play doctor or nurse and give you an enema, but it's really just a divine experiment to him, not a huge thrill. He needs to get out of his head (he is the biggest worrier and the most analytical of all Tauruses) to just enjoy getting good head like everybody else.

Third-Decanate Taurus (May 11–20): The Saturn Decanate

These Taurus men were born at the end of the Taurus season, and they tend to be late bloomers. They are influenced by the cardinal earth sign, Capricorn, which makes them the most ambitious, persistent Tauruses, but sometimes the least lucky. The Capricorn influence gives them a Saturnian edge. Saturn is the "tough love" planet. He teaches patience and the value of hard work and smart strategizing. Third-decanate Tauruses usually get "luckier" as they get older, generally because by then they have learned how to make their own luck. They are the most likely to end up being rich (a major goal of all Tauruses) and powerful (the Saturn influence).

In the romance department, these boys are definitely the kinkiest. Inside they believe they are bad and love to be punished, or to punish you if you try to be a bad influence on them. Their personal business cards should read, "Role-playing, specialty."

If You Have His Chart

By looking at Mr. Taurus's chart you can get some clues as to what he's like on a deeper, more specific level. We'll save the really deep and specific stuff for another book, darling, but here are some helpful hints.

If he has a fire sign rising (also known as the ascendant) in his chart, whether it's Aries, Leo, or Sagittarius, he is probably a bit more spontaneous than his other Taurus brothers. A lot of water in his chart (Cancer, Scorpio, or Pisces) makes him deeper, more sensitive, and much harder to understand. This kind of Taurus must trust you implicitly before opening up. Be patient with him and kind to him, and you will receive all that, and much more, in return.

If his Venus is in Taurus or Pisces, he is a lover built to last. Venus in Gemini makes him more fickle but a sexy kisser. Lots of air in his chart (Gemini, Libra, or Aquarius) will make this Taurus man more cerebral and intellectually motivated than your average Taurus. He is likely to trust his logic more than his primal instincts . . . don't let him: he is more irrational than he realizes!

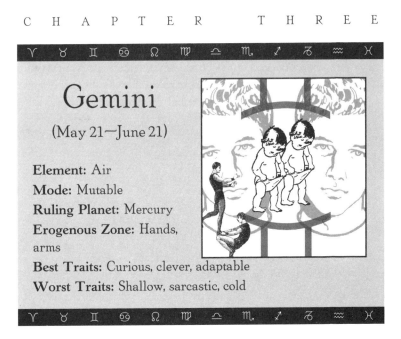

Gemini

(May 21–June 21)

Element: Air
Mode: Mutable
Ruling Planet: Mercury
Erogenous Zone: Hands, arms
Best Traits: Curious, clever, adaptable
Worst Traits: Shallow, sarcastic, cold

In Life

The Gemini gay man is tremendous fun to be around. He's read every book and magazine article and seen every movie and exhibit there is to see. And even if he hasn't, he can easily make cocktail-party chat about them for hours. The Gemini man is basically good-natured and just wants to have fun (like his female Gemini counterpart Cyndi Lauper). Is that such a crime?

Mr. Gemini has a quick mind . . . and I'm talking superquick. Unlike Mr. Leo, who is just waiting for you to shut up so that he can say what he wants to say, or Mr. Aries, who will abruptly cut you off, Mr. Gemini will simply tune out and go into his much more scintillating head, if you start to bore him. And the young chap simply detests being bored or *under*stimulated.

Because he is so clever, you may find him working in a profession that demands strong writing and/or communicating abilities. Hopefully he has a job that is in no way monotonous. You see, if he gets to flit from interest to interest and project to project daily, he is probably a *happy* Gemini. If he is stuck in a rut in his life, you may find him depressed and depressing to be around. When he feels trapped, he can downright mean!

Mr. Gemini probably discovered his nature early in life and has found ways to keep himself happily busy (and he can never be too busy). He probably reads all the time, and his tastes are no doubt eclectic. He can swing from "Betty and Veronica" to Proust in the blink of his blank "Little Orphan Annie" eye. He is so much more facile than everybody else that after a while he is sure to bore himself!

This man needs people, and he needs 'em bad. Being born under a mutable sign, he is extremely adaptable. In fact, he's quite the chameleon. He tends to get involved in the interests of his friends, lovers, and colleagues (and his family if he's really desperate . . . he's known them so long they *really* bore him). He is no snob, mind you. Just as he can go from reading or seeing trash culture to putting on a tux and acting like the stuffiest patron of the arts, he also loves to get a taste of different types of people. But the main thing he looks for is humor. He can dig the witty side out of the most seemingly tedious individual. That's what makes him so charming, and so lovable.

You see, even though the above description may sound like the thumbnail sketch of a shallow man (and he'd be the first to stand up and scream, "I'm just a big ball of fluff!"), he actually possesses a bigger heart than you might imagine. Mr. Gemini is the most open person in the zodiac. He can talk to anyone and relishes the opportunity to hear anyone's opinion. He challenges himself daily, though, and expects others to do the same. He doesn't even realize how inspiring he is.

In Bed

He's a hot little loverboy. The Gemini man knows how easily bored he is and naturally assumes that you might be of the same ilk. That's why he will go to almost any length to surprise you (and himself) in the sexual arena. He digs doing it in public places, in groups, in strange costumes, and in positions that would challenge any circus contortionist worth his salt . . . and that's all in one night . . . and probably during your first night together.

He's fun in bed and likes to go from one extreme to the other. He loves to laugh and enjoys a lighthearted romp. But he is always desperate to *feel* more, since he tends to live so much of his life in his head. That's why he is drawn to his dark side, and yours. Anything that will make him feel a little less empty and a little more *intense* is a turn-on to him. But if *you* are thinking of going to extremes, you'd better be just a tad subtle about it. Remember, he is always two people. The one right in front of you, and the smart, funny one sitting, legs crossed in the thin air above you, just like Endora from *Bewitched*, laughing at the situation. So if you are too locked into your role of Daddy, Prison Bitch, or whatever and come across as heavy-handed, then he may "check out" right in the middle of the best fuck of *your* life.

So show him something he's never seen before, but don't plan it too much. Be spontaneous. He loves that! And he also loves to be surprised and caught off guard. He may protest a little, but watch the way he rolls with whatever crazy, slutty scenario you throw at him.

And before, during, and after the actual act (or acts, I hope!), try talking. He is the most verbal boy in the galaxy and has no trouble processing a wild, dirty story you tell him, while listening to his answering machine screen his calls, all the while taking your manhood inside him. He also enjoys just hearing what you have to say in a tender moment. He's not soppy and sentimental, but he is sincerely searching for his soul mate or (dare I say it) "twin." The more you are able to communicate who you are and the more you prod him to share his inner self with you, the more chance you have of being his bedmate for life.

Of course it helps if you have stamina, 'cause he does. This boy's brain never shuts off, and his body tends to follow suit. He can come more in one night than most and expects the same sort of energy, imagination, and enthusiasm from you. So don't disappoint him. And remember, any place is fair game for him. He certainly doesn't just limit himself to the bedroom. You may miss the second act of a darling gay play you took him to see because his hands are busy giving you something *really* dramatic to concentrate on. And you may nearly have a heart attack when he unzips his pants at Aunt May's Thanksgiving table, and slips your hand into his lap, as you are (ironically) passing Grandpa the butter. It's all part of the sexual life of the most whimsically degenerate gadabout of them all . . . Mr. Gemini.

How to Seduce Him

So you've spied him at your local coffee bar, sitting alone drinking endless lattes and reading Oscar Wilde while listening to a mix of Janet Jackson and Brahms on his Walkman, and you want to get to know him in an intimate way? But every time you get ready to make your move, he seems to be talking to someone else . . . a cute waiter, a nice older matron and her nephew, a series of his pals who have seen him in the window and stopped in to say hi?

What do you do? What *do* you do?

Well, here's a tip. Give him the eye, and don't stop staring him down till he has to pay attention to you. It's too risky to just go up and talk to him, because he is a conversational whore and will literally talk to anybody. So how will you know he's . . . you know . . . interested? No, the silent seduction route is better. That way he can't overanalyze or criticize the quality and appeal of your so-called casual banter.

Once he is within touching distance of you, you can talk, although he will probably make a little joke or comment to you first, to test your ability to think on your feet. If you make the first comment, I suggest you go back and forth between saying nice, complimentary things to him and then cutting him down with sarcasm. It's exactly what he would do, and he loves to be beaten at his own game.

The conversation will probably go something like this:

YOU: Popular, aren't we?
GEMINI: Yes, are *we*?
YOU: I just came in for a cup of coffee, but I couldn't keep my eyes off you. You've got sexy hands.

GEMINI: They're not real. *(Take his hand and squeeze it in a manly way . . . you know, the way you boys do.)*

YOU: No, but your attitude is.

GEMINI: And so is yours, I see. You know actually, my friend suggested I come over and find out why you were staring at me.

YOU: I know. I'm psychic and I wanted to see if I could will you over here with my mind.

GEMINI: That doesn't make you psychic. It makes you a mentalist . . . or a mental case.

YOU: I bet I can tell you what you're thinking right now.

GEMINI: That's easy. Why don't you do something really impressive and bend that spoon?

Et cetera. You get the idea. To a Gemini this is "foreplay." And if you want to get him on his back, you'd better keep on your toes. It's hard work, but believe me, he'll show you his appreciation for your efforts.

Doing Him and Dating Him

If you read my last section (and you had better have, you ungrateful, selfish . . . oh, sorry . . . I thought I was up to the section about Cancer guilt, which is even worse than a Jewish mother's guilt), then you have probably already figured out that life with Señor Gemini is much like being on a television sitcom. Witty and light banter, compelling characters, and a lot of commercial breaks when you can . . . you know . . . do what boys do.

The Gemini man likes to prove himself in a sexual way, so he may spend most of his time trying to get you naked. However, what will really turn him on, once the initial conquests are over, is if *you* turn him on to new things. What can he learn from you? He's a quick study, so throw something challenging and unusual at him. He tells you he knows nothing (other than what he's picked up here and there) about homosexual love trysts in Europe during the First World War, which just happens to be what you're writing a book about. Well, enthrall him with your acumen, Agent Starling.

You spoke Russian fluently in high school, but have lost it over the years? Well, brush up and practice on him. He loves to learn and has a fantastic ear. And I hope for your sake you like his friends, because he will bring them along on your little dates (which usually have many parts to them including dancing, sex, renting a video, baking a cake, and scouting locations for his brother's film) whenever he feels like it. He's a divinely social creature, so you'd better be, too. If *you* start trying to possess him and keep him locked up in your bedroom or shower, away from the social and intellectual stimuli he needs to survive, then you can forget about making it to the next section.

How to Last over the Long Haul

Nice segue, huh? So, how does one last with the most easily bored man in the zodiac? First of all, try to understand him on a deeper level. Yes, I know I've painted a smart but flitty picture of him, but if I can call a gay Gemini man my best friend for nearly half my life, then you can make an effort to know him, with the same genuine interest his dear dyke friend would. And friendship is key, sweetie.

If you can put your own dirty, twisted agenda aside for a minute and try to get a handle on what makes him tick and what makes him happy, then maybe you will be lucky enough to be the old queen standing next to this Dorian Gray–like, forever young, sexy genius at his fiftieth anniversary party.

First off, you need to stop taking every mood of his so seriously and get some objectivity on yourself. He is really kind of a nervous guy. What do you expect from someone whose mind is always racing faster than the speed of cocaine, even without any illicit substances in his body? Don't you see that the dear boy needs the right balance of comfort and predictability combined with entertainment and open-mindedness? To paraphrase a famous hetero Gemini (perhaps a little *too* hetero?), "Ask not what your Gemini can do for you, ask what you can do for your Gemini." He is naturally giving because most things just aren't a big deal to him.

And unlike Mr. Capricorn, who will keep a running tab on all "fritter money" he lends you, or Mr. Pisces, who will keep an emotional tab running every time he lets you cry on his shoulder, Mr. Gemini gives naturally, with no strings attached. So try doing the same for him. If you've been around him long enough to see that he sometimes needs his space just to read or gab on the phone to his pals, then let him have those things without going all "Me! Me! Me!" on him. And if he is overworked because (as usual) he has taken on too many things at once, why not surprise him by sending a nice dinner to his office? You'd be surprised by how far just a little bit of thoughtfulness will go with him.

How to Get Rid of Him

Rule number one: don't treat him like a fool. It always sucks to be dumped, and he's played both roles—dumper and dumpee—many times. So he can handle it. But don't you dare take the avoidant route with him. Say what's on your mind. He's a talker and will probably want to "work it through." But if the fire is out, don't worry too much about him. He's got plenty of friends to dish you with, and he'll secretly be happy on some level to have the chance to experience someone newer and more interesting than you. Now do you feel as if *you've* just been dumped?

The Three Faces of Gemini

Every sign is broken up into three decanates, each of which gives the Sun sign a distinctive flavor. Keep in mind, though, that the Sun enters and leaves each sign a day later or earlier during different years. Make the proper adjustments for boys born on the cusp of their sign. Wipe that dumb look off your face and just do it. All right, you Geminis, no whining, just check an ephemeris and see what the exact dates of your (or your pal's) Sun sign were for the year in question, divide by three, and there you will find the correct decanates.

First-Decanate Gemini (May 21–May 31): The Mercury Decanate

He's the most Geminian of all Geminis. The early Geminis are the smartest, and the most nervous. It's all that extra Mercurial energy. He needs help finding his center, and staying calm. Get him to a meditation or yoga class but quick. This man may need an operation to get his brain to shut off! And in love, he can be the most fickle. He more than any of the other Geminis needs for you to constantly reinvent yourself and challenge him. Getting into a rut is torture to this man's soul.

Second-Decanate Gemini (June 1–June 10): The Venus Decanate

He's the most partner-oriented of all the Geminis. He likes being in a relationship, he likes having a business partner, and he likes having a buddy to talk to every day who will fill him in on all gossip, world news, and *New York Times* crossword-puzzle trivia. This Gemini is the least caustic and the least likely to enjoy an argument. He needs to be liked more than the others and is therefore the most likely to tone down his razor-sharp edge. Second-decanate Geminis can be quite artistic and are sensitive to their environment. This brand of Gemini man also appreciates the good life more than the others. He likes the feel of expensive fabric against his skin. Keep him in the style he's grown accustomed to.

Third-Decanate Gemini (June 11–June 21): The Uranus Decanate

The third-decanate Gemini is the most likely to want to help mankind (which is exactly what he'll tell his public while sporting a nice little Speedo at the local beauty contest). He is the most loving, yet has the most intimacy problems. He needs to learn relationship by relationship, friendship by friendship, that everyone wants more one-on-one time with him, which is the thing that he is most protective of. He wants to help the world, and I am quite sure he will, but he needs the most help in attaining the thing he wants most of all: true love.

If You Have His Chart

A look at his chart will give you a much more detailed idea of what this multifaceted man is like. If he has a nice dose of Cancer or Scorpio in his chart, he is probably a lot more emotional and intuitive than your average egghead of a Gemini. A nice bit of Taurus, Leo, or Aquarius makes him more focused than the typical queen born under the sign of the Twins.

If he has a lot of Gemini, or any of the other mutable signs (Virgo, Sagittarius, Pisces), he is probably a bit of a rambling man, and it may be hard for him to stick to one thing for years at a time.

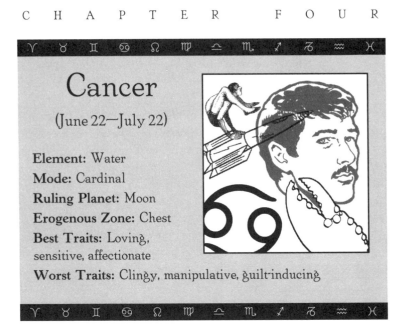

Cancer

(June 22–July 22)

Element: Water
Mode: Cardinal
Ruling Planet: Moon
Erogenous Zone: Chest
Best Traits: Loving, sensitive, affectionate
Worst Traits: Clingy, manipulative, guilt-inducing

In Life

Most gay men are looking for a daddy. But how many are looking for a mommy? A lot, actually. And that's why the Cancer man is so in demand when it comes to romance. Of course he can't always see it that way. He's earned his moody reputation, but his Norma Desmond–esque mood swings are actually quite natural, when you think about it. You see, Mr. Cancer is ruled by the moon, which changes signs approximately every two days . . . that's a lot quicker than any other planet out there. And with each sign change, you will see a different side of the Cancer guy. He can be a morose drunk, a brilliant artist, a savvy workaholic businessman, a hot lover, a nagging mother, and more . . . all in just a fortnight! Sound scary? Actually, it's not. If you are around him long enough (like, say, two months if you're very observant, and a lot more if you possess only average powers of perception), you will begin to see and understand the rhythm and mysterious but comforting pre-

dictability of his moods. Of course, you may feel as if you are dealing with a pregnant woman whose hormones are out of whack, but
if you have a few mother issues of your own (you *know* he's got
plenty), you should be rather turned on by the whole Cancer experience.

Mr. Cancer's wacky moods may at times convince you that he is
emotionally unstable or, to put it mildly, completely off his rocker.
In reality, he is just moody. Supermoody. But that doesn't mean he
isn't incredibly steady and capable in his dealings outside the home.
He is security-minded and probably has a nice, stable job. Even if
he works in a traditionally unstable field such as entertainment or
organized crime, he will still make his own regular and predictable
routine.

If you are dating him, you will see that he immediately gravitates
toward rituals: watch an old Rock Hudson or Tony Perkins movie
on Wednesday nights; have sex by candlelight in the bathtub at
midnight on Fridays, etc. He's sort of like an animal that way. He
likes his rituals and he likes to possess the things and people he
needs and desires.

Yes, he's clingy, but most people crave such clinginess. When
he's holding you in his arms late at night and reassuring you that
everything will be all right, you will feel just like Monty Clift did
when Liz Taylor looked into his eyes and said, "Tell, Mama," in
A Place in the Sun. Yes, when the sun rises and the world is less
scary, you may think, "I don't need this. I can do okay on my own,"
but even you will know that you're fooling yourself.

Everyone should experience the crazy romantic foolishness of a
Cancer at least once in his life—especially if you're a gay man (and
if you're not, why are you reading this book? Put it down and run
screaming out of the room!). And if you're lucky, you'll hold on to
this howling-at-the-moon-crazy Cancer queen for life.

In Bed

The Cancer gay man is so deliciously repressed that he is capable
of being the world's greatest lover and the world's worst (sometimes

all in the same day!). Cancer men in general have weird mother fixations that they refuse to deal with in their "real" lives, so it's no wonder they must work it all out in bed with you. "Oh, but gay men are so much less uptight than straight men, that can't be the case for my hot Cancer man," you say. Well, yes, sweetheart, your Cancer lover is more likely to feel comfortable wearing a ball gown doing his imitation of Madonna doing her imitation of Evita, atop a gay pride float, but that doesn't make him any less screwed up in the sack than his straight brethren.

He carries all the family guilt and shame around with him every day. It took years for him to get over the taunts and teasing and feelings of being "less than" masculine enough as a child. So, in bed he may overcompensate by wowing you with feats of manliness, which will prevent you from sitting down for days, or he could open up to you in a most erotic way and invite you to do every disgusting thing imaginable *to* him.

But the real glory that the Cancer man is capable of achieving, sexually, will come when he lets go of his last inhibition and allows himself to give and receive, to experience both his rough side and his tender side, his top side and his bottom side. His leather, his lace. You get the picture.

As for details, here are some things to keep in mind when you are alone with a Cancer man, a bunch of condoms and a roomful of cheering fans (oh, sorry, I thought I was talking about a Leo or an Aquarius for a moment there). First, remember his erogenous zone: his delicious and incredibly sensitive chest. Give those nips and pecs the workout they deserve. He loves to have his tits sucked on for hours. Yes, Virginia . . . like a woman. At some point you will want to break out tit clamps or other little doodads to make his pleasure complete.

He is also incredibly tender and cuddly, after the deed is done. The Cancer man is naturally affectionate, and after you've made love (I don't care if you got him off in a subway station men's room during rush hour, it's still "making love" to him, dammit!) he will feel as if he's come home. And home and family mean a lot to this man.

Atmosphere is also important. He enjoys a rough scene at times, but if you are seeing him as a lover, you should really pay attention to lights, music, and other sensual aphrodisiacs. This will bring out the best in him. He likes sex to have a fantasy-like feeling to it.

But once the fantasy is over, if you don't have the decency to act like someone he can bring home to Mother, than get your stuff and get out. He wants a whore in the bedroom, and a nice boy when the sun comes up. Can you be both for him?

How to Seduce Him

I hope you are looking for one of two things: a lifetime commitment or a one-night stand, because there is no in-between with dear Mr. Cancer. If you just want a quickie with him, be clear about it. Grab him and do him, and don't make a big deal about it later. And make the sex as dirty and "inappropriate" as possible; meaning, if there's a chance his boss or his father will walk in, all the better. If you are looking for love of the "forever" variety with a Cancer man, read on.

Rule number one: adjust yourself to his mood. Okay, you know he's a creature of habit. So at 1:00 P.M. sharp on every other weekday you know you can expect to find him buying a $35 salad from the deli/salad bar by his office (so he happens to like meat loaf, mashed potatoes, and other comfort foods in his salad . . . so what?). So you get yourself all psyched up to make small talk with him and you approach, confident but cautious.

Well, sweetheart, you may have noticed after stalking him, like a good little boy for several weeks, that he has a great sense of humor. You've heard him make jokes with shop owners and messengers. But the most important question you should ask yourself on the day that you are all dressed in your best trendy but respectable gay-boy outerwear is this: *What is his mood?*

If he is not smiling and is only making minimal chitchat, perhaps you had better steer clear of him or pour on the compassion. Pick up something sweet and gooey and give it to him as a "treat," 'cause "you look like you're having a helluva day." Then smile and extend your hand. Introduce yourself. Then make a gentle exit. If his mood suddenly changes, he'll perk up and ask you to have lunch with him. Or find out where you work and he'll come visit you. But if there is just no pulling him up from the depths of that day's depression, then I suggest you take a "less is more" approach. Let him brood over you a bit.

Doing Him and Dating Him

Do you like to eat? Do you like to stay home and cuddle in front of the TV? Do you like to have sex? If you answered yes to all of the above, then you are ready to start dating a Cancer man. And you get extra points if you can do all of the above at once. Mr. Cancer makes a great boyfriend. He is affectionate in public and in private, he is loyal and loving and will probably be the object of much desire from friends and strangers alike. Wait a minute . . . he could be a chocolate Labrador retriever, couldn't he?

Well, I guess. But can a dog discover what makes you scream with pleasure and give it to you as often as you want it? Never mind.

Sexually, he is ready to go at it almost anytime, but you may have to teach him a few tricks. He is not so imaginative sexually. He knows what he likes, and he likes it a lot. If you are simply burning to be straddled over the bathtub while he recites passages from the *Mommie Dearest* screenplay ("Don't fuck with me, fellas!"), then you'd better guide him into a suit that accentuates his broad shoulders and lure him into position yourself. He's resistant to change at first, but then once he feels comfortable, he's just as kinky as the next fashionable sodomite.

How to Last over the Long Haul

For someone who is so into having a lasting relationship, the Cancer man may surprise you with eleventh-hour "I'm not ready" speeches well after the two of you have made a commitment to each other. Don't let him worry you too much. It's just the simple fact that because home and family mean so much to him, he sometimes rebels against himself, out of fear that if he gets too comfortable, the rug will be pulled out from under him.

What you can do is to reassure him, reassure him, and reassure him some more. But if you have any fears and worries, I suggest you talk about them and pull his secrets out of him. They will be much less frightening to both of you during the light of day. But please be patient. You may have to put up with weeks of odd behavior and false "I'm fine" 's until he is ready to burst into tears and tell you what's the matter.

If you are willing to put up with his crazy moods and fun party game of "It's not me, it's you!" when you point out the inconsistencies in his behavior, then you will actually be in for a pretty fabulous relationship. The key to making it last with a Cancer man is simple. Get married. I don't care how you do it, but do it and stick to those vows. Come home every night and expect the same from him. Be loyal and loving and talk things through before stepping out or throwing in the towel. Start a family. And learn to deal with his family and your own.

Simple, but this is stuff that few people, homo, het, or dyke can actually manage to pull off in one lifetime. No hidden tricks here. But if you can put your relationship with him at the top of your list of priorities and demand the same of him, you two can set an example to us all. Anita Bryant and Jerry Falwell be damned!

How to Get Rid of Him

Well, you could move to another state and change your name. Not because he'll follow you and hunt you down (unless you count the first eighteen months after your breakup). No. You should move because you may not have any friends or family left. They aren't about to give up going to *his* house on Thursday nights for his famous eggplant lasagna with homemade death-by-chocolate cheesecake for dessert. Please, Mary! Be realistic!

If you are really sure you want out of this union, and you don't want to leave town, here's what you could do. Start treating him like a roommate, not a lover. Be nice, but not nice enough to give him the nooky he needs. Then introduce him to a new "friend." You know what he likes. You say his ideal man is a cross between Tom Cruise, Larry Kramer, and Nancy ("Jo" from *The Facts of Life*)

McKeon? Well, you go out and find that guy and make sure he ingratiates himself to your man. The only way to get rid of him is if you set it up so that he has a man to go to next. Let the new "Mrs. Cancer" provide the shoulder for your soon-to-be ex to cry on, over you.

Be kind but firm when you tell him it's over, 'cause he has a way of appealing to your innermost needs and insecurities. The man does not let go easily (even if you've only been going out for two weeks!). Good luck, my friend. And remember, there are lots of nice places to live in Bosnia.

The Three Faces of Cancer

Every sign is broken up into three decanates, each of which gives the Sun sign a distinctive flavor. Keep in mind, though, that the Sun enters and leaves each sign a day later or earlier during different years. Make the proper adjustments for boys born on the cusp of their sign. Wipe that dumb look off your face and just do it. All right, you Cancer boys, no whining, just check an ephemeris and see what the exact dates of your (or your pal's) Sun sign were for the year in question, divide by three, and there you will find the correct decanates.

First-Decanate Cancer (June 22–July 1): The Lunar Decanate

He is the *Canceriest* of Cancers. First-decanate Cancers are the most affected by the moon's transits (which, remember, occur about every other day!) and the most in touch with their "feminine" side. So that explains what's in his locked lingerie drawer! These early Cancers are supersensitive and supershy. Some may cover this up by developing outgoing "personas," but that's all they are. Deep down he's just a home-loving, completely emotional little sweetie pie. And if you ever question his manhood, he'll show you just what sweet stuff he's made of . . . with the back of his hand. These Cancers often develop into great leaders to make up for their fear of drowning in emotion. They have the most family complexes but make the best parents.

Second-Decanate Cancer (July 2–12): The Pluto Decanate

These Cancers are the sexiest and the most driven of all Cancers. They tend toward obsession and will focus on a goal or project with a fierceness that is rare and beautiful. These middle Cancer men are more resilient than the other kinds, but also the most brutal when they feel they need to be. There is a strong survival instinct here, and a strong need for power. You'll feel it when you're in bed with him. He will try to dominate you either physically, emotionally, or in both ways. This man wants *you* to be obsessed with him. In love, that is his goal. At some point in his life he will have to go to hell and back to find his soul. He's deep. He's fucked-up. And he's likely to be as popular as they come, for these middle Cancers are absolute charismathons.

Third-Decanate Cancer (July 13–22): The Neptune Decanate

This Cancer is the dreamiest and most imaginative of them all. The Neptunian influence of Pisces has shadowed him since childhood. He has secret fears and demons that he may never share with another living soul. But hopefully, if he is in touch with the artist or healer within him, he will find an outlet for those magical powers and psychic abilities that are both a blessing and a curse.

He's forgetful. How could he possibly remember his appointment with the chiropractor on Monday, and to pick up lemons and garlic at the store on his way home on Tuesday, when his mind is so filled with lyrical images and poetic visions?

Third-decanate Cancers are immensely talented but immensely vague. He really needs to be around people who will love him for his dreamy ways and vivid imagination, but who will help him to do something with his inner magic. He needs focus, or else the ghost of failure could haunt him and turn him into a bitter man. He's an old soul who feels most at home near the water.

If You Have His Chart

If you can get ahold of his chart (which might, oy vay, involve getting in touch with his nutty mother for a time of birth), you can understand him on a deeper level. Look to see if he has a good breath of fresh air in his chart (Gemini, Libra, or Aquarius). This will make him a little bit more objective and detached than your average Cancer.

A strong Pisces or Leo influence could bring out the artist in him. Lots of earth (Taurus, Virgo, or Capricorn) will make him even more of a homebody than usual (and that's saying a lot!).

A full ninth house, however, will take him away from his home and make him more of a traveler. So will an active twelfth house.

If he has moon in Cancer or a packed fourth house, you had better try to understand his mother almost as well as you understand your own, for she will be the greatest single influence on his life.

♈ ♉ ♊ ♋ ♌ ♍ ♎ ♏ ♐ ♑ ♒ ♓

Leo

(July 23—August 22)

Element: Fire
Mode: Fixed
Ruling Planet: Sun
Erogenous Zone: Back
Best Traits: Loyal, loving, good leader
Worst Traits: Bossy, pompous, vain

♈ ♉ ♊ ♋ ♌ ♍ ♎ ♏ ♐ ♑ ♒ ♓

In Life

Gay Leo men simply adore being Leos. They equate their Sun sign with grandeur, glamour, and gorgeousness. And they are right. Leo men lead their lives with a certain pizzazz. They are all movie stars on the inside, and most of them show it by the way they accessorize on the outside. They're all incredibly vain, which can be annoying at times, but endearing, too. After all, they want to make the world a more beautiful place. And if they have to buy themselves expensive jewels or hairdos to do so, so be it. If it was good enough for their heroine, the late lovely Leo Jackie O, then it's good enough for them.

In their careers, they tend to gravitate in two directions: the arts or big business. If they are the business type, you can bet that they are either in charge or on their way to being in charge. These cats don't like to take orders from anyone. Mr. Leo can be surprisingly conservative in business. He knows how to work from within the system and is the ultimate insider (like that famous gay American president Bill Clinton. You knew he was gay, but did you know he was a Leo? Kisses to Hillary!—JD). He hates to rush, so he doesn't mind gradually working his way up to the top, but with his charisma, chances are he'll get there fast.

If he's an artistic Leo, you won't find him slaving away alone in his garret. No, this boy needs attention and lots of it. He can't live without a constant high dosage of adoration. A compliment makes him come to life. And if you adore his art, he knows that means you adore him. Of all the arts, acting is the one that he is the most gifted at. He is a natural performer and can rope in an audience with his divine sense of timing and people pleasing. Of course, even if he practices a craft that has nothing to do with the stage or screen, he will somehow manage to grab the limelight. (See Warhol, Andy, another famous Leo).

The Leo gay man also possesses a great integrity and honesty. He needs to live his life in a way that he deems moral and proper. That doesn't mean he has anything against prostitutes or drunks. He has compassion and love for all. But at some point in his life, he will face himself and his own shortcomings and have to make some serious choices about how he wants to lead his life. He may be a materialistic whore, but he is an honest one.

In Bed

He likes sex to last a long time, for this man hates to feel rushed. Oh, he'll get a quickie in a back room if he has to, but his sexual scenario of choice would be a weeklong vacation on a tropical island. He loves to mix luxury with tackiness (like another of his heroines: Leo Madonna . . . it's easy to give lots of examples of Leo heroes, because Leos value fame more than any other sign). So don't be surprised if he has a heart-shaped picture of his cat hanging next to an original Modigliani in his bedroom. The dear boy is just full of contradictions.

When it comes to getting down, he can be quite the sexy, sensual lover. His sense of touch is extremely sensitive. Whether you're a trick or a true love, he expects you to worship every inch of his . . .

body. Mr. Leo will growl with pleasure and excitement like a big cat (or maybe that is his cat chiming in the with the sound of his snores). Chances are he'll want to get you off first so that he can lie back and enjoy the delicious time you will spend on him. Not that he's a lazy or selfish lover. He just knows how to get the most bang for his buck.

And he is indeed a fire sign, which means he likes his sex hot, and his emotional ties warm. If you're going out with him, you can expect a lot of gentle laughter and excessive affection in the sack. He really is a sweetie, except for those rare occasions when he thinks he's in his office giving orders. Once in a while you may hear him holler, "I said I want it on my lap by two! Do you see what time it is? Oh, sorry, honey. You're doing great! A real bang-up job!" He knows when to stop criticizing and start praising.

He also knows where to do the deed. Mr. Leo is a thespian, after all, and knows that set and costumes are key elements of any good performance. If he knows you're coming over, he'll set the scene complete with candles, mirrors, expensive champagne, mirrors, smooth grooves on the CD player, mirrors . . . you get the picture. The man likes to get a look at himself during every position. In fact, videotaping before a live audience is to be encouraged. He's loud and loves to wake up the neighbors with his booming baritone ex-clamations of "Oh my God!"

I hope you are planning on staying for breakfast, because Mr. Leo likes his sexual experience to be complete, with a beginning, middle, and end. Even if you aren't going to be together past noon the day after the deed is done, you had still better make a good show of being enamored. If you don't, he is apt to throw your clothes out onto the street and call the vice squad. Did anyone say "drama queen"? Like Glenn Close's "Alex" in *Fatal Attraction,* he "won't be ignored!"

How to Seduce Him

Seducing a Leo man is bound to be a great joy for both of you. None of the other men in the zodiac appreciate the ancient art of romance as much as Mr. Leo (except maybe Mr. Libra, but his main priority is snagging himself a husband!). Flattery, of course is the key. You can be as obvious and over-the-top as you want, because even if he suspects your motives and doesn't trust your intentions, he'll still admire your taste. But if you are looking for a lover, not just a conquest, I suggest you try the sincere approach. Fawning over his physical beauty and stroking his ego could lead to stroking other parts of him, but if you really want the whole enchilada, go after his heart—completely.

There is plenty you can praise about him. He's warm, smart, proud, and as charismatic as they come. He probably has fantastic taste in certain areas and hideous taste in others. Look for the good and skim over the rest. After all, not many men can recite all of Shakespeare's sonnets by heart, so just forget the fact that he can also recite all of Celine Dion's lyrics by heart, too.

Pull out all the romantic stops. Don't make your date "casual" unless you want him to write your name in pencil in his address book and erase it with a huge flourish the next day. Dress up. Bring him a traditional gift: beautiful flowers or a fine wine. Take him someplace wonderful. He loves the theater or the clubs. And expects an incredible dinner, too. Yes, even if he's a poor struggling artist, he knows how to live the high life. If you are looking for a cheap date, knock on another door.

Doing Him and Dating Him

So, you've snagged a Leo man, eh? Congratulations. I hope you enjoy talking on the phone. You see, most fellows can answer the question "How are you?" in a few minutes; Mr. Leo will take no less than a few hours . . . every time. You had better keep asking him or he will think you're neglecting him. In which case he will be forced to give *you* "the cold treatment," which is very chilly indeed. And believe me, you will not want to be on the receiving end of this twice.

Mr. Leo will probably put you through a few tests before he opens his heart to you. His mama told him to shop around, so he is likely to hold back a bit in the beginning of your liaison. Of course his version of "holding back" is likely to be quite transparent, if he really likes you. He wants a one-on-one, completely possessive relationship.

His possessiveness and jealousy will come through early on. If you want to insult him and ruin your chances with him, bring one of your exes who's now a good pal along for a group outing. He'll charm your former lover, then go home alone leaving behind only an icy "Ta" for you. You had better be prepared to treat him like royalty. Yes, this man is totally high maintenance, but if your love is true, it will be totally worth it . . . which brings us to:

How to Last over the Long Haul

Your Leo lover is invested in the ideas of "forever," "monogamy," and "till death do us part." He fancies himself quite the respectable chap and knows that with respectability comes responsibility, which he is capable of handling. So you see, when it comes to the big, important issues in a relationship, he's phenomenal. It's dealing with him day to day that can be a major pain in the ass.

He's demanding. He wants what he wants when he wants it and he wants it with a smile. Patience is not a virtue he possesses. Oh, he can wait, but his pride swells more and more—and closes him down at a rapid pace—the longer he has to wait for what he believes is his due.

And he's a big baby. If a coworker slights him in the tiniest way by day, you can bet he will come home and cry on your shoulder for hours about it (unless he has heavy Sag planets, which would make him much more oblivious than the average Lion king).

So how do you make it through the years with this man who is as loving and lovable as they come, but who also positively personifies the term *high maintenance?*

Well, you choose your battles. Learn to let the little things roll off your back, and go along with the program most of the time. Mr. Leo is possessive but not clingy and will respect you if you pursue your own interests. A little bit of space can give you just the practical distance you need to come back home later and enjoy him. You should also be comfortable or plan on getting more comfortable with your own feelings. He's a major emotional force and will want to talk about feelings and talk about them a lot. Let him help you to warm up and love yourself, as much as he loves you.

How to Get Rid of Him

The Leo man is so proud that getting rid of him is not really that hard, in the practical sense. If you tell him you no longer feel for him the way you did when you first fell in love, and if you let him see that for you the dream is dead, he will not put up a fight. But you had better be bloody sure you want out before you make any grand proclamations. Mr. Leo's supportive friends and family members are already lining up to tear you apart, dearie. He's loyal and is surrounded by loyal people who turn into mad dogs when he's been hurt.

Of course, even if he takes your "It's not you, it's me" speech well, and even agrees that the relationship is over, he'll still stalk you a bit. Not physically (like a Scorpio) or psychically (like a Pisces). No this fire sign will simply get all his little cronies to track your every move and report back to him. In addition, you will be kept up-to-date (in mysterious ways) about his latest comings and goings, which are bound to be grand and fabulous. You see, Leo men can be gotten rid of, but they will not simply fade away.

The Three Faces of Leo

Every sign is broken up into three decanates, each of which gives the Sun sign a distinctive flavor. Keep in mind, though, that the Sun enters and leaves each sign a day later or earlier during different years. Make the proper adjustments for boys born on the cusp of their sign. Wipe that dumb look off your face and just do it. All right, you Leos, no whining, just check an ephemeris and see what the exact dates of your (or your pal's) Sun sign were for the year in question, divide by three, and there you will find the correct decanates.

First-Decanate Leo (July 23–August 2): The Solar Decanate

These are the most Leonine of Leo men. First-decanate Leos are the most stable and the most immovable of all. The Sun has the strongest influence on him, and he is likely to be a true and loyal lover and friend. He is also concerned with his place in the world and will take his career seriously. These early Leo men are apt to be the most cautious and conservative when it comes to career matters, though. Even Mick Jagger, a first-decanate Leo, went to the London School of Economics before pursuing that *other* career.

In love, these Leo men are the most reliable. Just be aware, though, that he was in love even before he met you . . . with the concept of home, family, and *respectability*. This Leo fellow is the most likely to want children, and he'll make a damn good father, too.

Second-Decanate Leo (August 3–12): The Jupiter Decanate

These Jupiter-influenced Leos are more free spirited than the other Lions. These boys like to roam, and it will take them a bit longer to settle down. They are adventurous men who love to explore the world. Travel makes them giddy, and a trip to an unknown place is a surefire way to cheer them up when they are blue. They are less focused, however, than the other Leos, and they may never completely "grow up."

Second-decanate Leo men are real risk-takers. This Leo is likely to be the last one on the dance floor at five in the afternoon the day after a wild circuit party. He is prone to excess and can be accident-prone, too. This Leo man likes his sex the wildest and is the most afraid of commitment.

He may tend to latch onto other bad boys who will only bring him trouble. Yet the good luck of Jupiter is on his side, and he will eventually learn from all his wandering and develop a deep philosophy about life.

At some point in his life (hopefully when he's older and wiser) he will develop a deep sense of spirituality and will be drawn to teaching others, based on his life experiences.

Third-Decanate Leo (August 13–22): The Mars Decanate

These Leos make the best Leos and are most able to cope with what other Leos abhor: being alone. They are the most independent and determined type of Leo. These guys are self-directed and like to do things their own way. They are also the most macho. Dominating comes naturally to them, and they enjoy chasing after the most sought after man in town. Man, I say, not *men*. These boys know how to be true, but they will leave you pining by the phone if you give in to them too easily. They love a challenge, in life and in romance.

They are honest and possess integrity, but they do tend to make their own rules. Influenced by the combative, individualistic planet Mars, these third-decanate Leos are out to do nothing less than change history, and they will.

If You Have His Chart

He'll be more than happy to show it to you. Leos are proud and love to show off. Here are some tips to see what kind of a nut, I mean, what kind of a Leo you have hooked up with. If he has a lot of Gemini in his chart, like my dear Leo agent, Ralph Vicinanza, he's apt to be extremely articulate and refined, and more of a quick thinker than most Leos. A good dose of Aquarius in his chart means he's an extremist. His strong belief system rules his life. Heavy Libra or Taurus planets make him a real romantic. He will get even more attached than your average Leo (and that's saying a lot) and may confuse sex with love (how unheard of!).

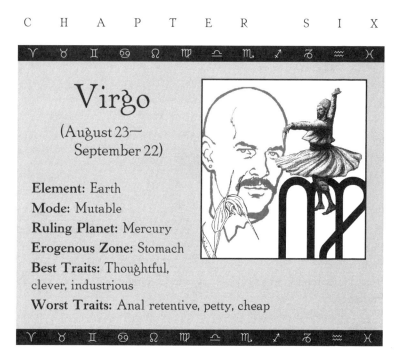

Virgo

(August 23—
September 22)

Element: Earth
Mode: Mutable
Ruling Planet: Mercury
Erogenous Zone: Stomach
Best Traits: Thoughtful,
clever, industrious
Worst Traits: Anal retentive, petty, cheap

In Life

Virgo gay men are quirky and unique. It's hard to generalize about them because the substance of their souls are so different. These boys, as a whole, though, tend to be sweet, gentle, and thoughtful, with a pronounced nervous streak. Virgo is a "feminine" sign (as are the other earth signs, and the water signs). This man doesn't have to wear a wig to know that he is just a soft, sensitive creature on the inside. Most of them emphasize some part of their personality or add something to their physical appearance to make them seem more manly, but it always seems just a little forced. Which isn't to say that he lacks true masculinity. He is just so evolved in his manhood that he is a little bit closer to the female experience than most men. This is why he has so many (biologically female) girlfriends.

Mr. Virgo prays to the God of work. He loves a project! And he loves to worry . . . especially about the details. He is an odd combination of the earth influence and the air sign influence of Mercury (Virgo's ruling planet). He sits on the fence between the physical world and the mental plane.

These men are incredibly bright and sensitive. He's really more of an escapee from a Victorian novel then he lets on. Even when they've been married for years, these guys still feel like humble spinsters on the inside. And humble he is. Some overcompensate, but all really believe they are "not worthy" of the grandiose things in life: you know, like love and happiness.

He is quite adept at language and is apt to work in a field that allows him to use his mind and his strong critical abilities. Virgo gay men also make good performers and editors (details, darling!). He must be happy in his work or he can't be happy in his life. He likes to feel a sense of purpose, and when he is appreciated by his boss and peers, he is at his best. The dear boy is hard on himself, and even when everyone tells him, "You're brilliant," and, "Your work is incredible," he will still say, "Oh, no, it's terrible," and pick it apart in minute detail. So you could imagine what he's like when he's working for someone who is never satisfied. He becomes a martyr and is absolutely no fun to be around.

Virgo men are often typecast as "clean freaks," "workaholics," and "nuts." He may be all of the above or he may be just the opposite. This man is prone to extremes.

Always remember that his greatest asset and his biggest Achilles' heel is his critical prowess. He may criticize the feng shui of your apartment, your use of syntax, and your homemade pasta, but it is only because he wants to help. You've no doubt heard what a perfectionist he is, and it's true. He believes life is a process . . . the process of making the world as clean and perfect and pure as his astrological symbol: the virgin . . . Mary!

In Bed

Mr. Virgo is so detail-oriented that even he has trouble remembering all the minutiae of his fantasies. Details and repetition are the meat and potatoes of his sex life. He is a lot more thrilling betwixt the sheets than his humble reputation suggests. After all, practice does make perfect, and Mr. V has been practicing his cute little sexual tricks as well as his huge, epiclike fantasies for years and years, since he was but a small Virgo pup.

Although he is a bit uptight in life, he definitely knows how to cut loose in the bedroom. He may ask you those tried-and-true questions "What do you like?" and "How do you like it?" Being verbal is not a problem for him. If you are shy and leave it to him, he will be really happy, for he has a myriad of scenes he loves to play out. Before that second margarita has hit you, you could be wearing a police uniform and doing something complicated with egg whites and handcuffs in his kitchen. If you do share a desire with him, perhaps a cigar-and-foot fetish, Mr. V will be able to call up at least 278 different positions and scenarios from his mental (or perhaps actual) card catalog. Leave it to him and the stogies and the smelly socks will be in place, and Mr. Virgo will give you all the dialogue you need to complement his well-memorized prose.

The man has a strong work ethic and you will know it, after the first hour of foreplay. He loves to take his time and extend the "act" for as long as possible. If it's hard for you to come, you are in luck (and so is he), for his favorite thing in the world is rolling up his sleeves and putting his nose to the . . . well, you know where.

It is less easy for Mr. Virgo to just relax and go with the flow, though. And he can be at a loss without his props (the right paddle, the right wig . . . you know). Since he is a mutable sign and a very communicative man, he is all right with following your lead. So if you want to take charge, he is fine with that. He is a man of many moods, though, so even if you do the same kind of things with him, time and time again, he will always throw in a different spin. And even when he's tired, he still finds a way to work up the energy to give a command performance. Just make sure that you show an interest in him, or else he will retreat to his favorite hobby: masturbation.

How to Seduce Him

Mr. Virgo may be a talker and a doer, but he is still rather shy on the inside. He will be flattered if you show an interest in him, and you'll be glad if you make a first move toward him. Don't let his prickly verbosity throw you. He is more insecure and in need of love and affection than he lets on.

Be simple and clear. If you just want to do him, then cruise him and ask him to come home with you. Just make sure your home looks decent. Don't get me wrong. He may very well be one of those Virgos who have such issues around cleanliness and dirtiness that they love to get really disgusting . . . from spit to scat . . . but you can never tell. So if you're pad isn't neutral enough (too clean makes him feel impotent; too dirty freaks him out), then go to his crib.

If you want to date him, then ask him out on a date. Coffee and something intellectual is a good way to start. Get cappuccino and get to know him, and maybe check out a reading or an exhibit. Stay away from the one thing that you can do with any other sign on a first date: eating. Mr. Virgo is a walking eating disorder. His stomach (which also happens to be his erogenous zone) is ultrasensitive, and he is a tremendous bore when it comes to explaining in tedious detail the "cans" and "can'ts" of his diet. So let him use his mouth for talking (and other activities, later), not consuming.

Doing Him and Dating Him

He's an eccentric chap. Mr. Virgo is a bit of a "confirmed bachelor" at heart . . . just like those handsome film stars of the fifties who never seemed to "get serious" about a girl! Well, he is sure about his sexuality, it's just dating and relationships in general that give him stomach pains. He has his routines and doesn't like to shake them up too much. Of course, he is likely to cover up that inflexible side of his nature when he first meets you. He may adapt to your routines and get more involved in your life than vice versa. However, he will always keep certain habits and routines of his, no matter how wrapped up in you and your neuroses he becomes.

Mr. Virgo is wonderful to talk to, in bed or out. When it comes to lovin', he can really handle criticism and is more open than he seems. If you have a want or a need, all you have to do is express yourself, Madonna, and he will go out of his way to please you. And during the light of day he is really fun to be around because his mind is so active. There's always plenty to talk about, and you will probably learn a lot from this soft-spoken man of inner strength.

How to Last over the Long Haul

As you have probably gathered by now, Mr. Virgo loves his compulsions, habits, and routines. His desire for repetition is what makes him a loyal lover. After all, he can find a million ways to sing the same song and a million ways to play the same flute duet, if you get my drift. So sticking with someone he loves is not a problem for him. What can be difficult is the fact that the dear boy is a slave to his routines. The most evolved Virgo men realize that they must grow in order to live up to the high standards they have set for themselves. So if you, O lover of Mr. Virgo, can help him to develop his talents and abilities and to challenge himself, he will forever be in your debt. And with all this growth and change comes new routines and neuroses. If you can support him in a new obsession every year or two, then you should be in good shape.

Ah, but what about *your* needs? Well, you can get Mr. Virgo to meet them if you are clear and consistent in the way you communicate your feelings to him. He's sort of like a Labrador retriever. He's easy on the eyes, smart, and loyal . . . but he's still just an animal! Therefore if you say "Down boy" in a different tone each time, you are likely to see him cock his head in confusion and cover his cock in fear. Consistency is a must, so don't give your Virgo lover mixed messages. If *you* are confused—about the relationship or other areas of your life—you should talk to him. He's a great listener because he is calm and nonreactive. On his own, he's a nervous wreck, but if you are vulnerable and nonthreatening, he's a real dreamboat.

And of course, the make or break of any relationship happens with the lights low and the clothes strewn on the floor, so here are some tips on how to keep the sex hot and the relationship steamy.

Don't let Mr. Virgo use sex purely as physical release. Push him to express some real passion. He desperately wants to, but when he's been with a lover for a long time, he does tend to treat sex like a good workout, and we all know how boring the StairMaster is after about two minutes. You should also develop a fantasy life together. He is bound to bring a million and one fetishes into the relationship, and you will probably bring in a few yourself. Why not create a scene that is unique and original for both of you? And why stop at one?

How to Get Rid of Him

When Mr. Virgo believes he is no longer needed or useful, he will go. If you've been with him awhile, you have probably grown accustomed to relying on him: to pick up milk (real for you, soy for him) on his way home from work, and to give you the foot massage that makes everything seem right with the world. Once you decline his offers of assistance, he will exhibit signs of depression, and from that point on it's just a matter of time. He may leave you first. Quietly and without making a big fuss. He may be relieved to go back to his lonely but somehow comforting bachelor life.

Of course some will not go without a fight. He may be the type that needs your help more than he will ever admit. If that's the case, be kind, for God's sake. Help him to find his way in the world without you. Help him to find a new routine. Be a friend to him. And then, once he is on his way, disappear, lie low for a while, and change your phone number, 'cause he is the stalker type.

The Three Faces of Virgo

Every sign is broken up into three decanates, each of which gives the Sun sign a distinctive flavor. Keep in mind, though, that the Sun enters and leaves each sign a day later or earlier during different years. Make the proper adjustments for boys born on the cusp of their sign. Wipe that dumb look off your face and just do it. All right, you Virgos, no whining, just check an ephemeris and see what the exact dates of your (or your pal's) Sun sign were for the year in question, divide by three, and there you will find the correct decanates.

First-Decanate Virgo (August 23– September 2): The Mercury Decanate

These boys are the most Virgoan of all Virgos, of course. First-decanate Virgos have a strong work ethic and a strong sense of fear. His challenge in this life is to use his fears to find his strength. Perhaps he is afraid that he is inarticulate. He may grow up to be an incredible writer or teacher. He must struggle with his personal demons more than the other Virgo fellows. He has the most secrets, and the most nervous habits. His mind works overtime and tends to play and replay events and conversations on a constant loop. He needs an outlet for all his anxiety, preferably something that involves athletics or talking or both. (Interpretive dance therapy, perhaps?)

Second-Decanate Virgo (September 3–12): The Saturn Decanate

These Virgos are the most career-oriented of the three. They may slave away for other people for years and then really come into their own, later in life. They are good planners and always land on their feet when it comes to money. They are more ambitious than they let on and always have a goal in mind. These boys are also the most prone to depression and often experience deep, dark nights of the soul. He will benefit from having a companion in life, for on his own he can become quite bitter and cynical. With love in his life, he becomes sexy, strong, and often *silly*.

Third-Decanate Virgo (September 13–22): The Venus Decanate

These Virgos are the most likely to be artistic and romantic and are less inhibited than the other Virgos. The Taurus/Venus influence makes them more peaceful and less nervous. They are social and creative, but oddly, can lack the famous Virgo sense of discipline. Once they discover what their passion is, they can be quite lively and joyful, but without that sense of purpose they are lost and may just follow their libido and their appetite for stimulation. These boys have more of a cast-iron stomach than the other decanates of Virgo.

If You Have His Chart

If you have a copy of his chart, you will find many clues to the kind of obsessions he has. And I'm sure he has many. A Virgo gay man with a lot of planets in Taurus and Leo could be quite the opera queen. A strong Taurus influence without Leo will just make him a major music aficionado, in general. A strong Scorpio influence makes him more serious and intense, with only two MOs in bed: fan-fucking-tastic and absolutely horrid. If Mr. Virgo has a lot of Libra in his chart, he is less likely to be so set in his ways and more apt to want to merge with a lover.

♈ ♉ ♊ ♋ ♌ ♍ ♎ ♏ ♐ ♑ ♒ ♓

Libra

(September 23 –
October 22)

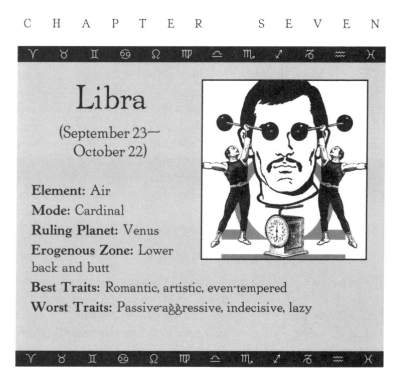

Element: Air
Mode: Cardinal
Ruling Planet: Venus
Erogenous Zone: Lower
back and butt
Best Traits: Romantic, artistic, even-tempered
Worst Traits: Passive-aggressive, indecisive, lazy

♈ ♉ ♊ ♋ ♌ ♍ ♎ ♏ ♐ ♑ ♒ ♓

In Life

The Libra gay man is first and foremost a real charmer. Ruled by beauty-loving Venus, he has a naturally gentle and calming way about him. With Venus being the planet of love, he is a true romantic. Since he was a young boy, he has imagined his life to be a fairy tale . . . in which he will be the star fairy, of course! He is full of dreams and whimsy, which he is extremely *unlikely* to express in words. In fact, many Libra men come across as quite practical, cerebral, and earthbound. Believe me, it's just an act. He had to butch up as a young man to compensate for his difference as a gay man, so the bullies wouldn't destroy him, and now as a grown-up he has become quite an impressive actor. He wants more than anything to be swept off his feet by the love of his life, and to live a storybook existence, making art and leading the life of the mind, and a life of luxury. Yet if he reveals all that, it will make him incredibly vulnerable. That's why he puts up some cold, chilly walls . . . to protect himself. But somehow his innocence and vulnerability shine through anyway, and they are his most wonderful traits.

Mr. Libra is also a great lover of art and probably a talented artiste himself. He has a great sense of the aesthetic. If he's an evolved Libra man, you will see it in the way he decorates. Even if he lives in a most humble abode, you can bet that the color scheme is subtly perfect and the lighting a dream come true.

If he does not pursue an artistic career, chances are he will do something that uses his highly developed sense of logic. Libra is the sign that rules law, but what does that have to do with logic, really? Of course he would make a divine lawyer, judge, or journalist . . . anything that calls for a strong sense of objectivity.

He's a funny paradox because on the one hand he is a true peace lover and diplomat (Mahatma Gandhi was a Libra; Jimmy Carter, too), but he just *loves* to provoke heated arguments. Then he sits back and watches the fur fly. He will never get blood on his hands, but he is often there on the scene of the crime when a big brouhaha is taking place. He's full of contradictions and his favorite hobby is switching sides in the middle of an argument. He's so charming, though, that most times he gets away with it.

In Bed

He's a sexy man, and he loves to be adored. Mr. Libra has highly developed pleasure centers, and you will no doubt experience a whole lot of joy as you discover each and every one of them. Of course, his sign does rule the ass, so you can imagine the fun you can have with that round and ready backside of his. His favorite thing to do in bed is to provoke you. He's the king of "I've been a bad boy." In fact, his routine is so rife with delicious clichés, you may feel as if you're a character in his private little porn flick. Just play your part well, darling, and he will, too.

Mr. Libra was born under the "masculine" air signs, so he's not *all* girl, you know! He can be a big top when he wants to be. He loves to find all the little things that drive you crazy and make you scream with pleasure . . . unless of course he's in a lazy mood, in which case you may get less bang for your buck. If you're going to be with a Libra man, you'd better train him right and treat him right. That means, invest in the fine leather costumes, good wine, and dinners out to get him in the mood for romance (the more money you spend, the more turned on he'll be!) and wrestle away the phone, his romance novel, or the remote control (if he has a lot of Taurus in his chart, this may be more challenging than you think) and make sure that sex is the only thing on his mind. Give him no out, and no option to change his mind. But do it lightly. Timing is everything with this man. Make sure you are paying attention to him and reading his signs clearly. Only this man, full of paradoxes and sweet surprises, could insist that you get rough with him but be more gentle about it.

He has a few modes in bed. The first is ultraromantic. This Venusian man is in love with love, and even if you've only gone on a few dates, I'll bet that he desperately wants to fall in love with you. So pour on the schmaltz. The right music and the sincere longing looks can do wonders for his libido. His second mode is intensely playful. Probably after you've been with him a while you will become his captive audience. That's when the fancy dresses and dance routines begin. And the third mode he gets into is (surprise) S/M. Mr. Libra loves being tied up, but then again, who doesn't? Any excuse to lie there and be ravaged is good enough for him. Of course if you're into getting thrashed a bit, he has no problem with that. He's classic and gravitates toward English-headmaster scenes. Yes, he is an Anglophile.

How to Seduce Him

Mr. Libra is easy to seduce because he's so . . . well . . . easy! Even when he's in a relationship, he enjoys dating. This boy was born knowing how to play both ends against the middle. He will let you know with his cute smile and come-hither glance that he is interested. His secret is the same as what young girls have been taught by their moms since the beginning of time: "Act interested, to get *him* interested." You'll feel as if you're on an interview during your first date. But it will be the smoothest and most subtle interview of his life. He may even take a page from fellow Libra Barbara Walters's book and ask, "What's the biggest misconception about you?" Don't be coy and make reference to your penis. The man appreciates good manners, so play the game, for God's sake. You can get nasty when it's *appropriate* to do so . . . which may not be till your second date. He likes to leave you wanting more.

If you ask him out, I suggest you do something that is somewhat theatrical or artistic. He's very opinionated and will love to sink his teeth into a nice debate about art or politics. And if you hold up your end well enough, then he'll sink his teeth into *you*.

Doing Him and Dating Him

Unless you've bagged a rich Libra, you should probably have a lot of money or the potential to make a lot of money before you get too serious with him. Oh, I'm not saying he's shallow, it's just that he lives by *my* mother's favorite saying: "It's just as easy to love a rich man as a poor one." The boy just likes to be *comfortable*. He lives for luxury, and for *lunching*. Surprise him at the office and take him out for lunch, and you'll win extra points. His fellow Venus-ruled sign, Taurus, sees God in the material things. Mr. Libra sees God in expensive skin cream, an expensive show, and a long, luxurious meal in a divinely atmospheric restaurant. His taste is exquisite and his yearnings many.

But you will get a lot in return with Mr. L. He loves romance. He'll brag about you and fawn over you in public and make you feel like the most important man in Canarsie (or wherever you call home). Yes, he is a not–so–subtle manipulator. But you'll put up with it 'cause he's so damn cute.

Example:

YOU: So, I don't get paid till next week, is it okay if we order in and . . . you know, get *comfortable*? We've gone out so much this week.

LIBRA MAN: Sure. I'm a little tired anyway. But I'll be happy to cook for you, if you're broke.

YOU: No, no. I just want to have a nice long night
             alone with you.

LIBRA MAN: Me, too. Why don't I cook? Then we can just
             watch some TV and act like an old married cou-
             ple. Next week we can go to that lovely little
             bistro on Fourth Street. Of course, all the cool
             people are there now, but who cares about that?

YOU: Oh, I don't want to be a drag. Why don't we
             just go tonight? I'll put it on AmEx.

LIBRA MAN: Oh, no. I'd much *rather* stay in. I'll put on an
             old bathrobe and start cooking.

YOU: Oh, you're too cute to slave over a hot stove.
             Let's go. I insist! My treat!

LIBRA MAN: Well, if you're sure that's what *you* want.

YOU: Of course.

LIBRA MAN: Great. You know that place *really* looks *sexy*.

And you'll know from his bedroom eyes that you will get the
fuck of your life after you drop some big bills at Chez Wherever.
You'll go into debt, but you'll live well.

How to Last over the Long Haul

Mr. Libra loves being in a relationship. He hates to attend any social
function alone, so having a boyfriend means he'll always have a date.
The challenge is in making sure it's *you* that he wants, not just any
man who looks good in a blazer. There is one big subtle trap you
must be careful of when you're involved with a Libra man. Make
sure that you don't suck him into your world and assume that all
the things you love, he loves, too. Mr. Libra is a born peacemaker
and consciously *hates* conflict. But unconsciously he sets things up
so that conflict is inevitable.

He may go along with you on everything or manipulate you into
doing what he wants (see previous example) the way a child whee-
dles a toy out of his parents, but at some point he will hit you with
an "I'm losing myself and feel trapped" speech. To avoid that mess,

you had better push him to really get in touch with what he wants and encourage him to be direct about his needs. Of course that can only happen once he's figured out what his needs are. And that's no mean feat, considering how long it takes him to decide just what tie to wear. But once you've trained him to train you how to be a good boyfriend to him, then you must hold up the other end of the bargain. Allow him to express his anger and express your own, *in moderation. Moderation* is a word the Libra man loves, whether he realizes it or not. He hates to take sides, so always let him have it both ways.

Of course, that does not include cheatin'. Oh, sure, you two may have a "trick on the side, with condoms" arrangement, but even that could be, well, tricky. The relationship a Libra man longs for is one in which he gets all his needs met. Well, that one ain't possible, but it sure is worth aiming for. Mr. Libra lives for the early days of romance, when flowers are bought often and sweet words are exchanged after a rousing roll in the hay. If you can keep the romance alive, you can keep him, and keep him all to yourself, which is exactly what *he* wants.

How to Get Rid of Him

He's pretty thin-skinned and loves the illusion of "perfection," so if you point out all the things that you hate about your relationship, you can pretty much kiss him good-bye. He could easily turn the tables on you, though, and pick up the first handsome stranger (or more likely, your best friend) and start a new relationship before you've even talked about moving out. The guy just can't bear to be alone.

Even if he's a more evolved type, he really does *hate* to be alone. So if you go out with your friends a lot and leave him home to eat by himself, talk to himself, and whack off by himself, he will begin plotting how to leave you without looking like "the bad guy."

If you want to be less obvious, you could simply fuck with his sense of order and harmony. He loves to eat by candlelight with Miles Davis playing softly in the background? Well, I guess it's time for take-out burritos seven nights a week with heavy-metal accompaniment. And while you're at it, rearrange his closet and leave his sexy velvet pants on the floor for the cat to nest on.

You can also pick on his real weak spot: his personal appearance. If you jab at him for his love handles, he will eventually use *your* credit card to buy some nice liposuction (it's too much work to go to a gym), get trim and toned, and go out and find a boyfriend who is cuter and richer than you are. You just can't win!

The Three Faces of Libra

Every sign is broken up into three decanates, each of which gives the Sun sign a distinctive flavor. Keep in mind, though, that the Sun enters and leaves each sign a day later or earlier during different years. Make the proper adjustments for boys born on the cusp of their sign. Wipe that dumb look off your face and just do it. All right, you Libras, no whining, just check an ephemeris and see what the exact dates of your (or your pal's) Sun sign were for the year in question, divide by three, and there you will find the correct decanates.

First-Decanate Libra (September 23– October 2): The Venus Decanate

Gay men born early in the Libra cycle possess the strongest Libran characteristics. They are apt to be the most artistic and the most sensitive of all Libras. They are especially in tune with their environment and need to live and work in places that simultaneously inspire and calm them. They hate to be alone and thrive when they have a partner by their side. That means in their love life as well as in their business life. Collaborating is especially fun and satisfying for them. Probably because it pushes so many buttons. You see, these Libra men are deathly afraid that they *can't* stand alone. Of course it's a baseless fear, but it's a profound one nevertheless. If, however, they choose the *right* partners in life, they will learn to stand on their own two feet. They make divine long-term lovers once they've faced their demons.

Second-Decanate Libra (October 3–12): The Uranus Decanate

The second-decanate Libra gay man is the most socially responsible. The Aquarius influence makes him more conscious of helping the world. He will have a strong desire to contribute to society. But he is more of an extremist than the other Libra men. When he is not out there trying to save the planet, he is likely to indulge in some heavily hedonistic activities. He's a bit of 1960s love child who likes to experiment with drugs and group sex. He has a great appetite for challenges and is likely to meet fascinating people and make some wonderful friends throughout his life. Yet, he will always struggle with a feeling of being alone. Oh, he doesn't mind being alone, or having space, in the day-to-day sense. In fact he likes to feel the wide-open spaces around him and revels in being the only man on the beach. But it is a feeling of being painfully alone, within the world, that haunts him. Experiencing true intimacy is especially hard for him. He is the most misunderstood of all Libras.

Third-Decanate Libra (October 13–22): The Mercury Decanate

The third-decanate Libra man is the most cerebral of them all. He needs a lot of mental stimulation all day every day. He's the chattiest and the most sociable. He has a light touch that makes him charming to all, but he can be a tad too superficial at times. He has a beautiful gift for language and should use it in his professional life. His lover must be entertaining and must enjoy being entertained, for men born during the last decanate of Libra simply live for a good show. These fellows often find great solace and great inspiration through reading. His mind is razor sharp, but he may shy away from soppy shows of emotion. He will challenge the people he is close to and will expect to be challenged back.

If You Have His Chart

If you have a copy of Mr. Libra's chart, you can find clues to the more subtle aspects of his nature. A gay Libra man with a lot of Scorpio in his chart is apt to be an intense lover who keeps a lot of secrets. Love for him means everything, but it also feels like a threat to his very survival. Complex! Libra men who have a lot of fire in their chart (Aries, Leo, or Sagittarius) are more aggressive than your typical Libra. This man is apt to have a lot of initiative and a hot temper (but it's unlikely he'll hold a grudge). Libra men with a lot of earth in their chart (Taurus, Virgo, or Capricorn) will crave more financial success than the average Libra. He will work harder and find success younger than most.

Scorpio

(October 23—
November 21)

Element: Water
Mode: Fixed
Ruling Planets: Pluto, Mars
Erogenous Zone: Genitalia
Best Traits: Emotional depth, charismatic, driven
Worst Traits: Domineering, secretive, extreme mood swings

In Life

Mr. Scorpio is intense and driven and there's no in-between with him. He knew from an early age that sex could be used as a weapon. Probably it was used on him in a threatening way. As a boy, he developed a sense of his own power and a fear of it, too. He can't help but suspect danger all around him because he knows just how dangerous people can be, especially people like him! Generally, gay male Scorpios come in two varieties: those who strive for truth and pure goodness (with a lot of pleasurable and sexy escapades thrown in, too!) and those who move primally from person to person, draining the power from others to enhance their own sense of power. In short, they are either good or evil. In the case of Mr. Scorpio I will not include my usual condition of "depending upon his other planets . . ." No. In this case, he's either one kind of animal or the other.

Ruled by Pluto, the violent planet of transformation, every Scorpio man will at one time or another battle with himself and come out on one side or the other. This battle will probably take place over time. This man invented the concept of "the dark journey of the soul." And it is a journey, baby. If he makes it to the good side, he's quite a force to be reckoned with, in the best possible sense. He's loyal to those he loves and fiercely protective. He's driven, funny, sexy, and confident with a strong and deep sense of intuition. If he doesn't war with himself and come out on the evolved side, he can be a most dangerous man to deal with, one who will destroy himself and others, without even fully understanding why he is compelled to be so violent.

If he has a purpose in life (and he almost certainly does), he will strive to achieve his goal, no matter how long it takes. Even the most evolved Scorpio men do have to wrestle with their dark side, though. He has a naturally addictive personality. At times he may turn to sex or drugs to soothe his hurts. But he is just as capable of purifying himself to the extreme. He may kick all his bad habits at once: from promiscuity to pot. That's just his way. So what does he do when he's not swinging on a pendulum between the forces of life and death?

Well, he's probably having fun somewhere, enjoying some verbal repartee with a challenging naysayer and a roomful of fans. Or he may be out taking classes, working out, or researching a pet obsession. The man knows how to live life to the fullest. And he is never at a loss for energy, enthusiasm, and emotion.

In Bed

He's a real powerhouse. His identity is closely tied in with his sexuality. In bed, he is intense and passionate. He doesn't take sex lightly, and neither will you once you go a few rounds with him. He generally has two modes. He may go right for the gusto and just enjoy getting down to business right away, or he may enjoy exploring every nuance of you and every part of your body, giving you and himself a big basketful of teasing pleasure.

Mr. Scorpio likes his sex dark and mysterious. At his best he likes to push the limits of pleasure and possibility. At his worst he is the ultimate control queen. When he's just tricking, he likes to pour the passion and the X-rated language on thick. As he gets to know a lover, he can show a surprising amount of tenderness and playfulness. He has the ability to lighten up when he becomes more familiar. But there is no question that Mr. Scorpio sees sex as his way into the world of the unknown, and he desperately wants to "cross over" to where no man has ever gone before.

He has no problem experiencing pleasure and is always in search of the ultimate blow job. If you can give him an incredible one and are willing to roll with his many moods, you could be his lover for life. Mr. Scorpio appreciates a lover who views sex as a deep, meaningful experience. Hey, man, if you're light or casual about it, he may mirror you and tone down his intensity, so as not to overwhelm you or risk being made fun of by you. But if you can handle him, he can change your world with his superhuman feats of sexual gratification.

In life and in bed, the boy does have control issues. If he doesn't know you that well . . . if you're a trick or at an early stage of dating him . . . he will want to be completely in control of the sex you have. That means, he decides where, when, how, and exactly *what* you do in bed. It may not be obvious to you, but believe me, he'll be calling the shots. The fun really begins when you get to know him more, and he starts to trust you. That's when he relaxes a bit and starts to open up. And when he's open, he's open to absolutely anything.

He was born with a detailed, psychic knowledge of S/M. He may have a preference for top or bottom, but deep down he's very switch-able. When it comes to raunch, he really digs a good dungeon scene. Traditional master-and-slave routines, complete with all the appro-priate fetish talk, and leather props, are like mother's milk to him. It nourishes him and makes his orgasm more intense, as it cleanses his psyche. The hotter the sex, the more clearly he can see what life is about. And for him, sex had better always be hot.

How to Seduce Him

As I mentioned, the Scorpio man needs to be in control, particularly if he doesn't know you well. So be careful not to cross his boundaries. Instead, encourage him to cross yours. He's like a mysterious and aloof cat. Approach him gently, but if he backs away, then let him come to you. Better to stay still when it comes to the sometimes dangerous Scorpio man and let him slink over to you, in his own way.

Once you're talking to him, turn on the sex appeal, but make sure you are at your most subtle and elusive. Scorpios love mystery, and open books bore them. He would prefer to poke his way into your secrets rather than have you spill them out upon first meeting. He, like his Gemini brothers, also appreciates a quick wit and a verbal challenge. If you are fast on comebacks and slow on revealing yourself, you will certainly intrigue him.

You can also be slow and mysterious in the way that you get close to him sexually. Touch him in a longing way, but then don't follow through. Make him purr, then see what he does next. But remember again that he is the one in charge during this game of cat and mouse. And if he's the cat, you know what that makes you, Squeaky.

Doing Him and Dating Him

When a Scorpio man enters your life, you will feel your pulse race just a little bit faster, and you will find that life suddenly becomes much less predictable. Get used to this level of giddy yet heavy fun, because it's only the beginning. Mr. Scorpio, if he's learned the lesson of Libra, the sign just before him, is actually seeking balance in his life, if you can believe that! Because it is so *not* a part of his nature to find true balance, that is why he seeks it out and craves it in a lover. He is hoping that you will be able to offer him the whole package: sex, love, friendship, commitment, security, freedom. Oh, he aims high, all right!

Don't let his overemphasis on sex and passion fool you. He really wants it all. So if you can show him all the different sides of you and hint at the range of meaningful roles you can play in his life all under the moniker of *lover*, then you can bet that he will stick around to see what happens next.

How to Last over the Long Haul

Mr. Scorpio is a high-maintenance character. He needs a lot of attention when he has something important to say. And he will want to pull all your secrets out of you as time goes on. He has a lot of energy and so must you if you want to endure the turbulent and sexy roller coaster of life with a Scorpio man. If you think relationships should be predictable and you just want to relax and have a good time, maybe you should get involved with a Libra. If you want to be with Mr. Scorpio forever here are some tips.

Push the boundaries sexually. Mr. Scorpio tends to get more inhibited as he settles into a routine, so force him to be the dynamo he was during the first few months of your liaison. Shock him with what you're capable of in bed. You won't be lying when you say to him maniacally, "You're going to thank me for this."

Teach him how to fight fair. Mr. Scorpio does have a tough streak. It's his survival instinct, which some people mistake for a dangerous weapon. You could even ask him, "Is that a gun in your pocket or are you just happy to see me?" You see, he has the primal need to protect himself at all costs and may be more threatening than he has to be, or at least more sarcastic. Don't take that shit. Show him the error of his ways and teach him how to get his needs met without stomping all over yours.

Put a high value on excitement. Mr. Scorpio is deeply serious but has a remarkably fun side. He's a thrill seeker even if he presents himself as supercontrolled and respectable. If you can loosen up and enjoy the rocky but rollicking ride of a relationship with him, you may learn a lot about living life as its meant to be lived: with zeal and fire.

Mr. Scorpio may be a water sign, which is why he is so emotional and intuitive, but he is definitely the most fiery of the water signs and lives life more aggressively and with more directness. Although he's a volatile character, he is also incredibly loyal and loving, once he's committed.

When he's devoted to you, you will feel as if a strong yet tender tiger is protecting you as you sleep at night. And then when you wake up in the morning . . . roooargh! You will surely feel his paws all over you. It ain't a bad way to live, but it ain't for the weak-minded.

How to Get Rid of Him

This is truly a daunting task if he doesn't want to go. First of all, he is a fixed sign, which means that once attached, he stays attached. And he's a water sign, which means his emotions run deep, much deeper than they seem even (and they probably seem as if they go twenty thousand leagues under the sea!). So if you think he'll be easy to say good-bye to, forget it. He'll go through the five stages of grief: denial, anger, bullying, begging, and then totally wiping you out of his life. Blaming yourself is your only choice (unless of course he's one of the Scorpio addict types who need a program or a good shrink more than they need you), as he will surely attack you if you don't. So cop a plea and beg for the mercy of the court when it comes to setting a penalty.

Of course the other approach is that of slow torture. It's a little like the classic film *Gaslight* (if you're a Virgo like Charles Boyer, you should be able to pull it off easily). You just play with his head, pull away, treat him as if he's crazy, and when he calls you on it, change the facts on him. You may be able to truly convince him that either (a) he's going crazy or (b) you are the cause of all his angst. Either way, he's likely to take off eventually when he realizes that you are not going to change or acknowledge the strangeness of the situation. But if you are thinking of leaving him, then you must already know what it's like to be with him: a minefield. So I advise you to step *very carefully* or else all your well-laid plans could blow right up in your face.

The Three Faces of Scorpio

Every sign is broken up into three decanates, each of which gives the Sun sign a distinctive flavor. Keep in mind, though, that the Sun enters and leaves each sign a day later or earlier during different years. Make the proper adjustments for boys born on the cusp of their sign. Wipe that dumb look off your face and just do it. All right, you Scorpios, no whining, just check an ephemeris and see what the exact dates of your (or your pal's) Sun sign were for the year in question, divide by three, and there you will find the correct decanates.

First-Decanate Scorpio (October 23– November 1): The Pluto Decanate

This is the most Scorpionic of the Scorpio men. He has to go to hell and back to get to his own version of heaven. He's the most charismatic, volatile, and exciting of the three decanates. He thrives on turbulence and lives on sheer willpower. When he is focused on something or someone nothing can deter him. He can also go through periods of extremes when it comes to sex: from hordes of lovers to complete celibacy. When he finds his comfort zone, look out, then nothing can stop him. A little bit of balance in his life brings out the best in this excessive character.

Second-Decanate Scorpio (November 2–11): The Neptune Decanate

He is the most imaginative of the three decanates. These middle Scorpio men are influenced by Neptune, the planet of illusion. They may be great artists, using the power of illusion to show the world something magical. They may also be great healers, another aspect of Neptune. But they can also be the most lost at times. They are so influenced by their powerful psychic abilities that they may be frozen and immobilized for long periods. When they make a commitment in their life to do something artistic, or to help mankind in some way, only *then* do they get in touch with their Plutonian drive and start making things happen.

Third-Decanate Scorpio (November 12– 21): The Lunar Decanate

These boys are the most relationship-oriented. Because of the influence of the homey sign Cancer, they really need to feel as if they are part of a family. They are homebodies at heart and enjoy the familiar. They are moody as hell because of the influence of the quick-moving moon, but their moods are actually predictable. They put relationships at the top of their list of priorities and truly need a mate in life. They are so nurturing that they are sure to have lots of suitors. More conventional than the other Scorpios, they can be assertive in their personal lives, more cautious in their careers.

If You Have His Chart

If you have his chart, you can get more insight into this complex and never-easy-to-understand man. A Scorpio man with a lot of Gemini or Aquarius in his chart is bound to be brilliant with a capital B. But, he is unlikely to let anything go by without challenging it. A lot of earth in his chart (Taurus, Virgo, and Capricorn) means that he is much more stable and volatile than your average Scorp, but much more hard to read, too. A healthy dose of Aries or Sag makes him much more fun than most serious Scorpios, but wilder, too. You will need to keep him on a long leash . . . literally!

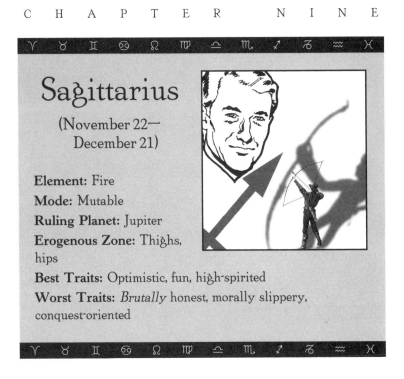

Sagittarius

(November 22–
December 21)

Element: Fire
Mode: Mutable
Ruling Planet: Jupiter
Erogenous Zone: Thighs, hips
Best Traits: Optimistic, fun, high-spirited
Worst Traits: *Brutally* honest, morally slippery, conquest-oriented

In Life

The Sagittarius gay man is the most adventurous man in the zodiac. He may go out and try to drink in as much of life as he can and experience the great wonders of nature firsthand, or he may prefer to read everything under the sun and use his imagination to fill in the gaps. Or if he's really evolved, he may do both. This man has a restless spirit, so it's no wonder he loves to travel. The typical Sagittarius man loves to try exotic foods, meet exotic people, and, basically, befriend everyone in the bar. He's generous, excessive, lucky, and a risk-taker. Unless he has some serious Capricorn or Taurus in his chart, the last thing he is, is practical.

This man believes in living life, not building up security or worrying about future rainy days. He is very in the now, which is why he always presents such a hipper-than-thou presence. Why, even the ones whose business cards read "Geek Personified" are on the cutting edge of every retro-nerd trend that rolls around.

Mr. Sag was born under the sign of the philosopher. He has a bit of the preacher in him, too. These boys can go to extremes when it comes to politics and religion. At one point in his life he may fancy himself a born-again Christian. At another point he may become an activist, who fights with all he's got to battle the Christian right. Yes, he's a zealot and a nut!

His biggest battle, though, is with his own integrity.

You see, most of these boys are tremendously lucky and early on discover the ability to slide through life. That could include fibbing to a lover about infidelity. "Of course I didn't sleep with that waiter! How could you even think that?" (All right, technically, a hand job in the men's room is not "sleeping together," but wouldn't it be more honest to just tell boyfriend dearest the whole truth?) Or he may become so palsy-walsy with his boss that he gets away with murder on the job and is the only one to get a raise when everyone else is being downsized.

Still, honesty is a major issue with him. Mr. Sag has the reputation of being "brutally honest." Yeah, he's the type who'll tell you, "Wow, your back is getting hairy, and that Grizzly Adams look was never in to begin with." Or he might blab to a roomful of status-conscious queens, "Hey, can you believe Bill only makes ten dollars an hour!" Charming. Yet, somehow this scalawag gets away with bad behavior. Why? Because he really is completely unmalicious (unless he has a lot of Scorpio planets). *Nothing* embarrasses him, so he can't relate to the feeling. Feel like shaving your pubes in front of him as you watch the eleven o'clock news together? Fine. Your boyfriend said you suck in bed? No biggie. Nothing fazes him, and he loves to laugh at life. Because he can laugh at himself, people usually laugh with him, not at him.

He really, really wants to be an honest man, but unfortunately he can resist anything except temptation (and a delicious ass). As he gets older, he begins to realize that he has to become the best ideal of himself that he can be or die a broken, hollow man. He will struggle his whole life with these issues, though. But a worthwhile struggle it is, for Mr. Sag desperately needs to discover and define the terms of his life philosophy. And he must set an example with his own life. Along the way of course, he may act like the most insufferable, charming, and naughty bad boy you've ever met in your life.

In Bed

Mr. Sagittarius is passionate and fiery. He fancies himself the smooth Latin lover (even if he's Irish), but may not be fully aware of just how goofy he is. No matter how old or experienced he is, he will always maintain an extremely cute and boyish sexual persona. This boy likes to play. As a lover he is randy and rambunctious. Most will try anything once, and if they like it, they will start a very public fetish organization to announce to the world how much they dig, oh, say, backseat humping while driving (no easy feat . . . although most do have big feet that can reach the gas pedal).

He loves to be spontaneous. Even if he's been with a lover for years, and they both have busy bicoastal schedules, he still can't bear the idea of making what married folks like to call "a sex date." He's old-fashioned that way and prefers jumping his main squeeze at the most inappropriate time and place.

He's still just a big teenager, no matter how old he is, and loves the thrill and danger of "being caught." Public sex, outdoor sex, and sex in strange places are particularly appealing to him. And if you are not in the mood, he loves the challenge of turning you on.

The guy also likes threesomes (or moresomes). He's a complete exhibitionist who finds it exciting to perform for an audience. So if you have a video camera, for goodness' sakes, whip it out.

Of course, since being faithful is not his strong suit, you may have to put a tail on him to make sure he's not fucking Mr. Third Party behind your back. Mr. Sag is compelled to break rules and push limits, and he will probably try your patience.

He likes to play games and may give you a costume to bring to bed. He may have several props tucked under his pillow, too. Or he may just enjoy a friendly game of strip Scrabble (he loves pursuits that are physical *and* mental).

As I mentioned, he is excessive. He likes a big seven-course meal before loving, during, and after. Although most Sag guys are skinny throughout their youth, they tend to pudge out as they get older. They are just great hedonists, that's all. And that same large appetite makes them wonderful lovers.

But he is certainly a sincere and avid lover, who believes that sex is the most life-affirming act in the world.

How to Seduce Him

Better to let him seduce you. He loves a challenge and may take what's given to him too easily for granted. Tease him and drive him wild with promises without committing to anything concrete. Wait before you hop into bed with him. Or at least, leave during the middle of the night with one of those "gotta get up early and do the crossword puzzle" excuses. Challenge him. He knows that he charms his way through life and appreciates a man who can call him on his ruses. Make an honest man out of him, and he will be forever attached to you.

If you are wondering how to get his attention, here's a suggestion. Find out his obsessions. He doesn't make a secret of them. If he's a Hong Kong–movie fan, show up at a John Woo festival and make small talk with him. If you can argue with him and show that you have strong, brilliant (and totally irrational) opinions, he'll be impressed. He doesn't want someone to agree with him. He wants someone to make him rethink all his well-crafted, impassioned arguments.

Doing Him and Dating Him

The first thing you should keep in mind when beginning a liaison with Mr. Sag is that his biological clock is different from everybody else's, and I ain't talking about having babies. He loves to stay up late and party. He closes down the house, after having made pals with everybody at the club. He's a good-time boy. Remarkably, he's able to get up the next day and go to work, then slip off to the gym around five-thirty, only to hit happy hour and do it all over again.

He's got energy and endurance to spare, but do you? Well, you'd better get some.

He is also *not* very big on intimate "alone" time. If you're having fun eating dinner together, wouldn't it be even more fun to invite some friends and strangers to join you? And while he's calling for extra chairs, he is unconsciously bringing together people who may *hate* each other. He loves free entertainment!

It's a loud, high-energy ride, dating Mr. Sag, but one that may make you feel seventeen again, no matter how old you are.

How to Last over the Long Haul

He's a wanderer, so I will be honest: hanging on to this rambling man over the long haul will not be easy. Number one, you've got to be flexible. Not only does he like to break rules, he likes to create new ones. He's not a tyrant like Mr. Aries or a bully like Mr. Taurus, but he is insistent on learning through experience, and growing and changing along with the times. Not a bad thing; it may just be hard for you to feel settled. If you are looking for a predictable mate, this ain't him.

You will probably want to develop your own independent streak. You have a nine-to-five gig but yearn to paint? Your Sag boyfriend may inspire you to pick up a brush and just do it. All of a sudden you're busy painting from 6 P.M. to midnight? He won't mind. He'll meet you for a late supper and dancing afterward. The more *you* pack into your own life, the more respect and love he'll have for you.

Mr. Sag must be allowed his freedom to explore the universe in his own way. If you boys can talk about what the "rules" are, great. Or perhaps you will just keep him on a long leash, and he will know instinctively how far he can go without jerking *your* chain too much. But you must realize that the man can't and won't be held down. He wants to experience life to the fullest, and if you stand in his way, he'll rebel against you and either make your life miserable or just plain leave. Don't ask him to change, but expect and demand that he be the best he can be. Your role, should you choose to accept it, is much like that of an army sergeant or a Peace Corps supervisor in charge of a young trainee. And it could be the toughest job you'll ever love.

How to Get Rid of Him

Force him to sign a legally binding contract (or at least one based on five parts Jewish guilt and five parts Catholic), and demand that he stick to it. Make sure he feels obligated to spend every waking moment with you, and then don't talk to him except to whine or nag. This fella hates to feel constricted, so if you box him in, he will find a way out. He's rather Houdini-esque that way.

You can also make a big deal about fidelity and brainwash him into being true to you, while you skirt around all over town. Of course, if you do this, you may find yourself in a morally ambiguous position, which Mr. Sag will be sure to preach to you about.

If you want to take the high road, then work as hard as you can to work it out with this well-meaning but often infuriating and wonderful man. If it's over, it's over, but be sure you promise to stay friends, and mean it. He holds friendship up to a much higher standard than romantic love.

The Three Faces of Sagittarius

Every sign is broken up into three decanates, each of which gives the Sun sign a distinctive flavor. Keep in mind, though, that the Sun enters and leaves each sign a day later or earlier during different years. Make the proper adjustments for boys born on the cusp of their sign. Wipe that dumb look off your face and just do it. All right, you Sag boys, no whining, just check an ephemeris and see what the exact dates of your (or your pal's) Sun sign were for the year in question, divide by three, and there you will find the correct decanates.

First-Decanate Sagittarius (November 22– December 1): The Jupiter Decanate

They are the Saggiest of all the Sagmen. These boys need to go down the wrong path before they discover the right one. They are fun-loving troublemakers who have a love-hate relationship with the truth. At some time they will work in publishing or as a preacher. They (not so) secretly see their own word as the gospel. They are accident-prone danger lovers who love the great outdoors, or they are at the other extreme and prefer to see the light of day only when absolutely necessary. First-decanate Sag men often have to wrestle with their consciences. They are a handful, even to themselves. But sexy . . . oh, yes, very, very.

Second-Decanate Sagittarius (December 2–11): The Mars Decanate

These middle Sag men have more focus than the others. Early in life they showed a pioneering spirit. Hopefully, that spirit was encouraged. For if it was, they have grown up into men who possess an overwhelming passion for life, and a sense of what the one (or two) things in life they really want to do are. They are more like loners than the other Sag men and need to find their own way, before they can settle down and mate with another (although they never settle down in a staid way). They crave to do something incredibly important for humanity, and to do it *first*. They probably will. These guys are lucky and brave, a dangerous and intriguing combination.

Third-Decanate Sagittarius (December 12–21): The Solar Decanate

These boys, born during some of the best shopping days of the year, are *extravagant*. The Leo influence makes them want to live large. They are great lovers and (once they've sown their wild oats) are much more loyal and stable boyfriends than most Sag men. They live for attention and love to have a microphone pointed at them. Perhaps an early association between a microphone and a man's phallus played a part in making them into some of the most media-savvy queens to walk God's green earth. They are compassionate and loving, and more than a little naive. They are the true innocents, and that's what makes these lads so beautiful.

If You Have His Chart

If you have a copy of his chart, you can get a more detailed picture of this extreme character. If he has a lot of Gemini in his chart, he *really* possesses a dual nature. A strong Libra presence makes him more romantic. Scorpio rising brings out the sexy monster you may be afraid to love but can't help falling for. If he has a strong Aquarius influence in his chart he could be brilliant but antisocial. A heavy-duty helping of Pisces makes him fearful and intensely sensitive.

♈ ♉ ♊ ♋ ♌ ♍ ♎ ♏ ♐ ♑ ♒ ♓

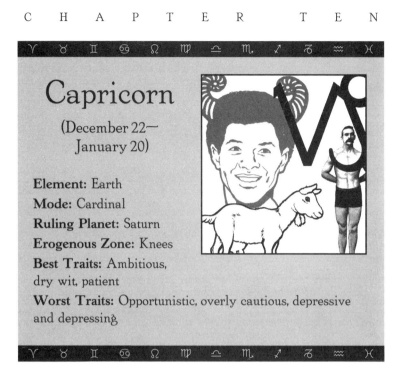

Capricorn

(December 22–
January 20)

Element: Earth
Mode: Cardinal
Ruling Planet: Saturn
Erogenous Zone: Knees
Best Traits: Ambitious,
dry wit, patient
Worst Traits: Opportunistic, overly cautious, depressive
and depressing

♈ ♉ ♊ ♋ ♌ ♍ ♎ ♏ ♐ ♑ ♒ ♓

In Life

The Capricorn gay man is a complex character with a simple view of the world. Success is his primary goal, and he will do whatever it takes to achieve it. Depression tends to stand in his way at times. Even though this man is funny and sharp, he can also totally lose his sense of humor when he begins to panic about his career. These panic attacks come and go in waves, but believe me, when he gets scared or blue, there is nothing much that can snap him out of it.

This man's Sun sign I see as being closely related to that of his opposite sign, Cancer. You see, Mr. Capricorn is at his best, and his happiest, when he can move on a steady forward course, but when the planets shift in ways that throw him off course, he can either rise to the occasion and go with the tide or sink into deep, dark waters of his own making. While Cancers, who are ruled by the moon, must get used to their mood swings and eventually find a way to groove with nature, Mr. Capricorn is too practical to believe in moods, feelings, or astrology. Well, he may go for the study of the stars, once he realizes he can plot a more successful course for his future by using this ancient blend of art and science.

You see, Capricorns are ruled by the stern and stoic planet, Saturn. Saturn is known as the great teacher. It teaches us all to make our own luck, not to rely on outer forces, but to develop ourselves; to strategize and to develop self-discipline. Yes, Mary, that makes Saturn a heavy planet and explains why Mr. Capricorn feels the weight of the world on his shoulders.

Lucky for him, life tends to get easier as he gets older. Probably this is because he has spent years developing wisdom and learning how to work hard and go after what he wants. But, oh, those black moods of his.

As a gay man he possesses the usual outlets for tension: obsessively going to the gym and sexually compulsive behavior. For the more evolved Capricorn gay man, there are other options. First, he should admit to himself that work is his God and set up his life so that he can achieve the career status he so desperately desires. Then he can focus his energies around this singular goal. For instance, if he wants to be a lawyer, he can study law, meet men through online legal/anal-sex chat rooms (two great tastes that go together), and contribute to his community by doing some pro bono work for immigrants with HIV or for bias-crime victims. The *content* of his work, whether his goal is to be a lawyer, a beautician, a plumber, or an actor, should be the glue that holds the rest of his life together.

If he is so out of touch with himself that he believes "Oh, work isn't that important to me" and "Moderate success is all I need," then I pity the poor boy. He will then take his frustrations out on his friends, family, lover, and most of all himself. Luckily, even a misguided Capricorn will eventually see the light and realize that his destiny is to be a mogul (nutty but fascinating and *rich* Capricorn Howard Hughes) and a role model in his chosen field (martyred hero to all activists Dr. Martin Luther King, Jr.).

And if you're a Capricorn looking for queer role models, how about the bisexual bombshell Marlene Dietrich. Just be careful, boys, that on your path to success you don't follow the road of the destructive closet-queen Capricorn J. Edgar Hoover. Although, one must admit he did achieve the Capricornian goal of supreme power in his lifetime, but all you goat boys out there must ask yourself, at what cost? Then create your own road to the top that's paved with ambition and *integrity*.

In Bed

Capricorn gay men are surprisingly earthy and fun in bed. They are so pent up all day, working, scheming, and plotting their own success stories, that they sure have a lot of steam to blow off by the time they are ready for lovin'. Capricorn men are earth signs first and foremost, which means that they are actually in their bodies during sex, not in their heads or in a fantasy world. They are right there with you and feeling every touch and kiss.

In truth they do like to receive more than they like to give, but these boys were raised to be diplomatic and negotiate, so you, you big dumb lug, may never realize what is going on. Mr. C may spend a long time teasing you and rocking your world, knowing full well that payback will be bliss. He just can't stop strategizing!

But this man brings his world-weary heaviness into the bedroom, too, and I see this as a good thing. He's been around the block. Even the young ones have experienced a great deal of pain and struggle, and so their pleasures mean even more to them. There is something bittersweet and intense about making love to a Capricorn man. His soul comes out in rare moments (and I'm sure you can guess which moments those are), and you will get the rare honor of seeing him with his guard (and his pants) down.

And while we're on the subject of pants down, don't forget to pay attention to that most unusual erogenous zone of his: his knees. His lower legs are sensitive, too. A tender stroke of the hair on his shins will send shivers up and down his body.

A little rough sex will do the same thing. Most Capricorn men have a paddling fetish. They're used to being the tops, simply because they're so good at delegating authority, but in reality, they love to spanked and whipped and punished for being bad. You can be tough with him. Ruthlessness and relentlessness are concepts he understands.

How to Seduce Him

What can you do for him? That's the question you must ask yourself before you even think of going after a Capricorn man. His theme song is that Gwen Guthrie club classic "There Ain't Nothin' Goin' On but the Rent." That's the one with the mantra "No romance without finance!" Yes, money is important to him. But unlike with Leo men, you don't have to spend oodles to impress this low-key earth-sign man. It's connections and power that are aphrodisiacs to him, not luxury. Take him to a cool little bistro, the kind that's located on a sweet street, with no sign outside. If you're pals with the maître d' and can get a perfect table on a Saturday night, you will certainly win points with your Capricorn man. And if you don't know the host, then slip him whatever cash (or other form of payment) it takes to get what you want. Persistence and resourcefulness are character traits that most every Capricorn possesses. Get in touch with those traits in yourself if you want to win this man's affections.

Even if your own goals (and means) are respectable but humble you still have a chance with the Capricorn man. If you make his goals your priority, you can pretty much guarantee a place in his heart and a place in his bed.

Doing Him and Dating Him

He's fun to go out with—when you can get him to go out. As you can see if you've come this far, Mr. Capricorn is married to his work. And if he is in a vague or unsatisfactory place in his career, then he will probably be married to his depression. Either way, your mission is to make the boy laugh. Capricorn men have a heavy and serious side that dominates their personalities, but these boys sure know how to have fun, too. Bring out his sense of humor and irony and you will get him to loosen up and enjoy the ride, instead of just obsessing about the destination.

Certainly you should respect his nature, though. He likes to brood and he likes to work and feel useful, so don't expect him to take a spontaneous, happy-go-lucky attitude toward life (unless he has a bunch of planets in Sag).

You *can* however teach him to get more in touch with his pleasure zones. Early in the relationship especially, Mr. Capricorn will be the most open to having fun and trying new things, from unusual sexual positions (some deemed physically impossible) to exotic foods. If you're intimate with him, you have the ability to help him to grow, which he will always be indebted to you for. And this man always pays back his debts.

How to Last over the Long Haul

Since Capricorn men are serious and don't like to waste their time, the question will inevitably arise from him, "Where is this relationship going?" He's old-fashioned, okay? He wants a ring on his finger and money in the bank. And he also likes to call the shots. If you've been together for a while, and he asks you point-blank what you want, you'd better be honest, because he will take you at your word and hold you to it.

If you are both on the "let's stay together" page, great. Now what? Well, be patient. Capricorns do not move quickly. Everything with these men is measured and weighed heavily. Your main challenge is to get him to reveal what is in his heart and to trust you. He is not a man who trusts easily, and if you want to gain his confidence in a significant way, you've got to earn it. With him, it is truly what you do, not what you say, that counts. Nevertheless, your word had better be gold, honey.

Take his needs for security seriously; like his earth-sign brother, Taurus, the Capricorn man does not like the feeling of being tied and tethered to nothing but the hand of fate, for he does not believe in good luck. And he shouldn't. The good luck he receives comes little by little and by his own hand, generally.

You had better be stable, reliable, and fun enough to make him laugh when he is feeling (and acting) martyred.

How to Get Rid of Him

Spend his money extravagantly. He'll love that. Quit your job. Go on the dole. You get the picture. All these things will make you pretty darn repugnant to him. If nothing you do makes him want to leave, then honesty is probably the best policy. Let him know it's over in no uncertain terms, as this is a guy who needs to know the bottom line. If you care about him and want to be kind, then keep in secret contact with his friends and make sure they are taking good care of him. He can be a tragic figure when he's in mourning. He may either throw himself completely and totally into work or forget to get out of bed and get dressed for weeks on end. Make sure he's in good hands—and leave him with a comfortable settlement. Even during the depths of his depression he can summon up the strength to say, "The couch is mine."

The Three Faces of Capricorn

Every sign is broken up into three decanates, each of which gives the Sun sign a distinctive flavor. Keep in mind, though, that the Sun enters and leaves each sign a day later or earlier during different years. Make the proper adjustments for boys born on the cusp of their sign. Wipe that dumb look off your face and just do it. All right, boys, no whining—just check an ephemeris and see what the exact dates of your (or your pal's) Sun sign were for the year in question, divide by three, and there you will find the correct decanates.

First-Decanate Capricorn (December 22–31): The Saturn Decanate

The most Capricornian of Capricorns, these boys are funny, savvy, and ambitious. They have a strong sense of family and community responsibility and often want to get ahead so that they can give back to others. They are sensitive and serious and possess a more feminine quality than the other decanates of Capricorn. These boys have a poignant intensity and strive for true sincerity. Nobility is in their blood. Like all Capricorns, however, they like to be in charge. Because they were born so close to the sign Sagittarius, many of them possess the Sag traits of integrity and preachiness. They are good leaders, even though they possess huge reserves of fear. Fighting for what they believe in helps them to overcome the terrors that haunt them at night.

Second-Decanate Capricorn (January 1–10): The Venus Decanate

These middle Capricorns are the earthiest and truly the most fun. They are highly sexual and pleasure-oriented (compared to the other Caps, that is). They are most likely to pursue artistic or athletic careers because the Venusian influence of Taurus makes them more inclined to be creative, and the superearthiness of the Bull's sign makes them more in touch with their bodies than the other Capricorn boys. They are strong and resilient and can weather the many storms of life. They make the best (or at least the easiest) lovers, as they appreciate stability and enjoy sex with the same partner regularly. These guys strive for simplicity in life.

Third-Decanate Capricorn (January 11–20): The Mercury Decanate

These humble fellows enjoy work for work's sake. The Virgo influence makes them less self-serving but more self-righteous. They like to throw themselves into a job and lose themselves in the details. They are responsible and smart. The quick-thinking influence of Virgo's ruler, Mercury, combined with the natural Capricorn gift for diplomacy, makes them great public speakers. When they say they are going to do something, they mean it.

If You Have His Chart

A copy of his chart will you tell you much more about your Capricorn man's personality . . . and his secrets . . .'cause they all have them. A strong Scorpio influence makes him sexier, more relentless, and more obsessive. Lots of Taurus in the chart makes him even more hung up on money and security, but at least he's open about it. Gemini rising makes him good with words and languages and more of a social creature. Lots of Cancer in the chart, particularly moon in Cancer, gives him strong ties to his family and a big old mother complex.

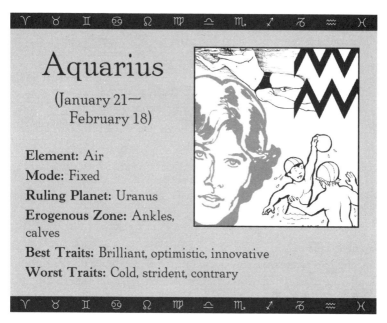

Aquarius

(January 21–
February 18)

Element: Air
Mode: Fixed
Ruling Planet: Uranus
Erogenous Zone: Ankles,
calves
Best Traits: Brilliant, optimistic, innovative
Worst Traits: Cold, strident, contrary

In Life

The Aquarius gay man is ahead of his time. He knew he was different at a young age. Different because he's gay, and different because he's completely bizarre. Many Aquarian men experience the sensation of watching life as if they are outside of their body. Yes, some of them are crazy, but most of them are just so profoundly detached that they are able to separate not just from the rest of the world, but from themselves, too.

Aquarius men tend to live in the future. They have great belief that the world of tomorrow is going to be much better—much more fair and humane—than the world of today. And most of these brilliant thinkers will go on to do great works, to *make* the universe a better place for all of us. These fellows can be awe-inspiring.

They can also drive you crazy if you're close to one of them. Intimacy is not their specialty. Aquarians are more comfortable with *we* that than with *I*. I'm not talking about the grand *we* of Leo. The Aquarian *we* can be very distancing, even when these well-meaning men use it to express loving concepts.

Example:

AQUARIUS: We *all* matter, don't we? We're all human beings!

YOU: Of course, but what about me?

AQUARIUS: Don't be selfish. Think about all of us.

YOU: But we started by talking about just the *two of us*.

AQUARIUS: Well, it's gotten bigger than that.

All right, students, does anyone have any idea what Mr. Aquarius is talking about? Yes, Rick? You have no idea? Good! Neither does Mr. Aquarius.

You see, Mr. A gets so caught up in ideas and concepts that involve "the world" that he has a hard time communicating one-on-one. He is also, as you can see, incredibly cerebral. His mind is his greatest asset and worst handicap. His ideas are bigger than life and idealistic, and his ability to think rationally and to reason are incredibly well developed. Often, however, his overactive brain cancels out his feelings. It's hard for him to just listen to his feelings and act on them. Even on the occasions when he does, he may talk himself out of it halfway through.

So what saves this poor, gifted soul? His friends. Friendship is the most important thing to Mr. Aquarius. It's a thing of beauty and inspiration to this highly gentle man. The Aquarian who chooses his friends wisely can count on them to pull his more emotional side out of him, and to teach him to deal with people he loves on a more *personal* level.

At heart, these men are scientists who seek deep and thorough understanding. From this place of knowledge they desire to change the world for the better. The challenge for Aquarian men is to understand how to relate to the people closest to them, using their hearts, not their heads.

In Bed

Experimental. Experimental. Experimental. Mr. Aquarius loves to try new things. He's a most nontraditional lover, who enjoys using the latest technology to enhance your orgasm and his. Video cameras help him enjoy the romp, and so do any sex toys that take D batteries. He'll try anything once, and if he likes it, he'll invite a few friends over to watch or participate.

Oh, yes, he loves groups. Just as he prefers to think in terms of *we* emotionally, he has the same tendency sexually. *"We* want to be tied up" or *"We* are going to cover every inch of you in chocolate and lick it off." Of course the "we" he refers to here is himself, his best friend, Steve, and Steve's lover, Michael. The "you" is you, his lover, and your friend Mario, and your accountant, Luis. When it comes to making love, the more the merrier, in Mr. Aquarius's world.

Getting a sexual rise out of him is easier than getting an emotional response. He's a cool character and needs a lot of space to feel safe. So if you drown him in intensity, you could scare him off. He needs to have his feelings coaxed out of him gently. But coax you should, or else you may feel that you are making love to the Sharper Image catalog of electronic paraphernalia.

When you are alone with him, he may surprise you with his passion and with his ability to communicate a thousand desires. When feeling enamored, he gives off the light, bubbly, and absolutely magnificent aura of fine champagne. Sex with an Aquarian is rarely heavy and is always a grand experience.

His fantasy life is rich, and he sure does like to act out many a kinky scenario. But at the heart of all the action and adventure is a deep desire to find a brother, a fantasy brother in the form of you, his lover, who will take him to the heights of sexual ecstasy. This man does believe in soul mates, and he sees his as someone who is one part protector/teacher and one part rival/challenger. And if you are all that as well as completely sexually uninhibited, then you are truly his ideal.

How to Seduce Him

Take off your clothes. Mr. Aquarius is a nudist at heart, and he may join you. Generally, the best way to get to him is by appealing to his body or his mind. Leave the heart and soul for later. He will be turned on if you have a free and easy approach to sex, and if you act a bit like an animal. He's so in his head most of the time that he will be relieved and fired up if you bring out the beast in him.

If you can reach him on a mental plane, too, all the better, for that is the playing field he is most at home in. If you have a lot in common but can still argue (sans personal attacks) the finer points, he is sure to be intrigued by you. And that intellectual intrigue will go a long way . . . all the way to his bedroom.

He may be smart, but he's still gullible enough to fall for an obvious seduction ploy. Tell him you have a theory (just the word is an aphrodisiac to him). You believe that two men can't sit on a couch together naked and watch porn without touching each other. Before you know it, you'll be tied up and watching *Cowboy Chicken Slave* on a loop and getting your cock sucked. Of course, Mr. A does have a sick sense of humor, and a huge interest in the political world, so you may have to suffer through hours of CNN before getting that one-on-one attention from him. It will be worth the wait.

Doing Him and Dating Him

Mr. Aquarius is funny about relationships. He desperately desires a hot lover to express his physical side with and yearns even more for a man whom he can talk to and find a true and magical meeting of the minds with. It's his *emotional* resistance that makes him so darned difficult! Mr. Aquarius needs his space almost as much as, and in some ways more than, his Gemini brothers. With the exception of the Libra tribe, who are in love with love, air signs as a rule are freedom- and space-loving folk. Charming and superintelligent as they are, it makes it hard to get an emotional read on them.

If you are getting involved with an Aquarius man, you must train yourself not to take his moods, comments, or most of what he says and does too *personally*. His nature and his goal in life are a scientific type of objectivity. Of course, his loved ones (including you, boyfriend dearest) will train him to stop being so extreme about his egghead theories of objectivity, since they do not apply *at all* when it comes to human beings! However, this is his nature, and it does make him a gentle and calming sort of fellow when he is not driving you crazy with his incredibly *im*personal theories about life and love.

How to Last over the Long Haul

Mr. Aquarius has a love/hate relationship with the whole idea of relationships. He's nonmonogamous by nature, so you may want to really hash out *that* fun issue before exchanging rings. He loves to communicate, so if you let him know it's safe to be honest, he will tell you what he really thinks and feels.

The two keys to making it last with this fascinating but often frustratingly intellectual man are (1) to keep experimenting in bed, and (2) to keep the friendship part of your relationship going strong.

The kind of understanding that this caring man has with his friends is what he wants with his lover, too (although he may not know that at times). And the key to his friendships is honesty. So while you two boys are being so honest, how about asking him what he really wants in bed. Some Aquarian men are shy at first (especially if he has Cancer rising or moon in Capricorn), but he'll tell you, all right. And it will probably be something that will completely shock you.

He's uncanny that way. He could become boyfriends with the toughest leather man in San Francisco and a year into the relationship confess, "I really want to whip *you*, Daddy." It has something to do with wanting to break taboos (yours) and an inexplicable, Uranian desire to be contrary.

He likes to expand his repertoire sexually and will consider it a real victory to help you get over your inhibitions (whether you want to or not!). You'd better play if you want to stay with him, and I'll bet you'll be happy you did.

How to Get Rid of Him

Argue with him regularly and refuse to listen to reason. Throw his "being contrary for the sake of being contrary" routine right back at him, but do it in a *personal* way. Invade his space, and above all, keep a closed mind.

Is he gone yet? I thought so.

If you want to get rid of him without being sadistic and cruel, you can tell him the truth: you'd rather be friends than lovers. He makes a great friend, and even if he's hurt at first, he will probably be the "bigger person" (he loves that!) and will come around to share platonic love, or at least "like," with you, later on down the road.

And since he's such a fantastic friend, *you*, my friend, will undoubtedly change your mind and will want to be his lover again. Too late!

The Three Faces of Aquarius

Every sign is broken up into three decanates, each of which gives the Sun sign a distinctive flavor. Keep in mind, though, that the Sun enters and leaves each sign a day later or earlier during different years. Make the proper adjustments for boys born on the cusp of their sign. Wipe that dumb look off your face and just do it. All right, boys, no whining, just check an ephemeris and see what the exact dates of your (or your pal's) Sun sign were for the year in question, divide by three, and there you will find the correct decanates.

First-Decanate Aquarius (January 21–30): The Uranus Decanate

Early Aquarians exhibit the more extreme characteristics of their sign. They tend to be the most idealistic, strident about their views, and the most intense about their friendships. These guys are ahead of their time. No question. But they may have a tough time finding their way in the world if they don't find an outlet for their passions. They are obsessive by nature, so if they have a constructive place to focus their fixating energy, we will *all* be a lot happier. These men can truly save the world if they can get their own lives together first!

Second-Decanate Aquarius (January 31– February 9): The Mercury Decanate

These Aquarian men are the brainiest of the bunch. The smart and quick-witted influence of Mercury makes their minds work faster than 90 percent of the population. Their problem, of course, is that they may live too much in their own heads and not enough in the real world, with other real people! They are a lot of fun, though, and are terrific at parties, because they love to chat about every obscure and fascinating subject under the sun. They're big flirts, too. These boys may have more than one career in their lifetime, as they have too many interests to just focus on one.

Third-Decanate Aquarius (February 10–18): The Venus Decanate

These Aquarian men, born during the last days of their sign, tend to be the most romantic and artistic. The refined influence of Venus brings out a softer side than one sees in the earlier Aquarians. These fellows are more subtle communicators and more capable of seeing the shades of gray than first- or second-decanate Aquarians. On the downside, they are much more impressionable and indecisive. A good marriage brings out the best in them. They are more likely to deal well in a monogamous relationship than the other Aquarians.

If You Have His Chart

If you have a copy of his chart, you can get a more in-depth sense of your favorite Aquarian man's nature. If he has Venus in Pisces, he is supremely giving as a lover, though he may want to "save" the man of his choice. Leo rising or moon makes him gloriously charismatic, though self-righteous, too. Lots of Scorpio in his chart? He's brilliant, but, boy, does he have his work cut out for him. He's too intense for his own good, but a truly unique and powerful individual.

♈ ♉ ♊ ♋ ♌ ♍ ♎ ♏ ♐ ♑ ♒ ♓

Pisces

(February 19—
March 20)

Element: Water
Mode: Mutable
Ruling Planet: Neptune
Erogenous Zone: Feet
Best Traits: Compassionate,
imaginative, intuitive
Worst Traits: Manipulative, escapist, passive

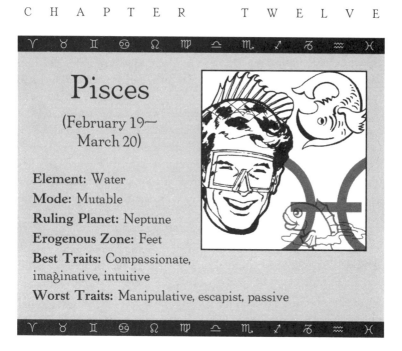

♈ ♉ ♊ ♋ ♌ ♍ ♎ ♏ ♐ ♑ ♒ ♓

In Life

The Pisces gay man has so many subtle colors in his palette, it is hard to know where to begin. The phrase that best describes this complex and kooky man is *imaginative healer.* Both qualities—the ability to heal and power of imagination—are closely associated with Neptune, his ruling planet. Neptune is the planet that is most closely linked with magic, and magic is something that every Pisces man believes in. The straight boys may be in denial, *of course,* but the more "in tune" gay Pisces boys know that a world of illusion comes alive every time they close their eyes to dream.

These fellows are just so damn vivid! Some Pisces men work in professions that are linked to healing or helping. They make great social workers, are drawn to hospital environments, and have a literal "healing touch" that they use to help the aged or the sick. You can expect to see many a Pisces man on the front line fighting for the rights of people with AIDS.

These men are almost always gentle by nature, but just watch them do battle when it's for a cause or, more likely, a person they love. They are activists in the most personal sense. It's not just "political" for them.

You can also find gay Pisces fellows working in the arts. Their imagination knows no bounds, which is why they make great performers, writers, and artists. The lucky ones tap into their story-telling abilities early in life and develop their gift for *not censoring* themselves. That's what makes their art so pure, emotional, and immediate. Some Pisces men struggle to fit their talents into the "real world." It's not easy, but if someone believes in them, they can make it.

Pisces men are so deeply sensitive and emotional that almost all of them run the risk of substance abuse, sexual addiction, or involvement with an active addict. Being born at the end of the zodiacal wheel, these guys all have a world-weary wisdom, which they at times try to deny. No wonder it feels easier for them to do a shot, pop a pill, or fuck till they can't remember who they are, rather than to deal with the pains of the world that they are supersensitive to.

Their environment affects them deeply. They can psychically sense the mood in a room, and they absorb it. Being so damn mutable is not easy for them. They often search for a calm, stable place to settle down in, but they soon realize that they will carry waves of feeling and fear with them their whole lives.

Their biggest challenge is to bestow some of that huge, all-encompassing Piscean compassion on themselves.

In Bed

Pisces men have the most in common with prostitutes of all the signs. That's right. They are complete and total whores. They love to act innocent on the outside and then show you just how bad they really are once you're all alone with them. The thing is, you know right from the start that they are about as innocent as a porn star. These guys have been around the block and probably started their sexual exploring when very young. If you think you started young, ask them. They'll shock you, then turn on that sweet Piscean charm. You'll think butter wouldn't melt in his ass . . . for about two minutes. Then you'll remember, this guy has (to paraphrase Charlene) "been undressed by kings and seen some things that a gay man ain't s'pposed to see."

The challenge for Mr. Pisces in bed is how to make you, his lover, feel special. Sure, he'll turn you on by doing *anything* you want the first dozen times. But then you'll probably start to feel a little bored. I mean, does he do this with all his johns? Yes. He does. That's when his brilliant imagination should kick in. He'll be called upon to top himself (in a manner of speaking) with you. To try some new tricks that he hasn't tried with other tricks before. Hopefully, he won't have to be bombed out of his mind to come through. If he is loaded with happy drugs, be careful. He'll crash eventually, and probably in someone else's bed.

So, what can *you* do to please him, to drive him absolutely wild? Well, to start with the obvious, pay attention to that famous erogenous zone of his: the feet. If he seems in the mood for romance, give him a foot massage that goes on for days and wait that long before you fuck him. He loves to be tortured by someone who does it well. If he's in a raunchy mood (more likely), then start worshiping his stinky feet or force him to do the same with yours. It's time to pull out the cigars, uniforms, and butch talk, baby.

The key to having the most fun in bed with Mr. Pisces, and crossing over into truly magical territory, is to start acting out some fantasies. He's a gifted role-player, although his are really all variations on the same two roles: (1) bad-boy, submissive bottom, and (2) raunchy, rough top daddy.

Ah, yes, now you see that the Thai-prostitute persona he played on Tuesday is not so different from the naughty British schoolboy he introduced you to on Thursday.

How to Seduce Him

Pisces men are without peer when it comes to the art of cruising. They can pick you up or be picked up anytime, anyplace, any day. The more obvious and inappropriate you are, the better.

Sitting in a Sexual Compulsives Anonymous meeting? Pass him a note to meet you in the men's room in five minutes. He'll be there.

Taking the GRE? Look him in the eye and then lick the shaft of your No. 2 while he is trying to figure out a logic problem. You'll get your man.

Out dancing with some guy you are just so *over?* Feel up your soon-to-be ex-boyfriend on the dance floor while you blow tongue-licking kisses at Mr. Pisces at the bar.

The point is, he is outrageous, so you'd better be, too. This man loves to break taboos. It's what he lives for. So don't disappoint him by being overly "appropriate."

Of course, once you have his attention, you should show a little emotion, too. He'll sleep with you even if you are a cold bastard, but he'll hang around if you've got a big . . . heart.

Doing Him and Dating Him

The most wonderful thing about Mr. Pisces in the early stage of a relationship is also the most frustrating thing about him: he is a crazy, romantic fool! He believes in love at first sight, which is sweet and endearing, and incredible, too, during this cynical age. But you may feel slightly uneasy with the way he professes to "know" you before you've even spent two weeks together. He falls hard and fast and wants to get to the emotional intimacy right away. Straight, no chaser. But it is precisely this rush to true love that should bring up a big red flag for you: perhaps he's not as comfortable with intimacy as he professes.

If you really do dig him a lot, then be the more mature lover, for his sake and yours, and force him to slow down a little, so that your "love" doesn't burn out within a month.

You could also try to spend some quality time with him that isn't sexual. He knows that sex is his greatest weapon and his strongest defense, so don't let him use it on you all the time. Hang out with him and his friends and see what his life is like. That will give you a better sense of whether he is stable, has done some therapy, isn't an active alcoholic, is a genuinely evolved Pisces man, or is a drunken whore without a job or a life.

How to Last over the Long Haul

You know that you have to keep the fantasy part of your sex life alive. Luckily, he is apt to do most of the work in that area. You know, too, that you have to keep your antennae up to see if he is actively acting out his latent compulsions for drugs and anonymous sex.

But the main area to dig into if you want to keep your relationship going for years is his secrets. Mr. Pisces believes his deep, dark secrets are worse than anybody else's. And who knows, he could be right. He is a truly kind and compassionate man, even though he has suffered a great deal in his life. That is what makes him so magnificent. He was probably abused to some degree as a child or young man, and from these horrible experiences he has learned empathy for others. He would never judge you, even if you told him that you'd committed murder. He can forgive anyone . . . but himself. This man carries around a lot of deep shame, and if you can find a way to open him up and get him to reveal his wounds, you are worthy of being his lover. And once those wounds are open, darling, you had better be prepared to help heal them, just as he has helped to heal yours. If you're lucky, you will learn about empathy and the real meaning of life and love, by helping this imaginative healer to heal himself.

Just keep the narcotics locked up before you venture over to his dark side.

Once you have gained his trust by making an attempt to open him up, then you should explore the more joyous side of his psyche: that famous imagination of his. Throw yourself into his world of art or magic and learn something about your own talents or powers.

You should also help him to function better in the concrete world. Mr. Pisces is divinely *im*practical. He is too lost in a fantasy world to know how to make a financial plan for the future (that isn't based on a pipe dream) or how to make the dreamy vision of what he wants to do with his life come to fruition in the mundane world. Be a source of support and guidance to him. He needs someone in his life who will inspire him emotionally, but help him in a practical way. If you can do both, and also enjoy degrading him in bed, he's yours for life.

How to Get Rid of Him

This is a tough one because Pisces men are so genuinely masochistic that if you are mean or cold to him, he will probably grow that much more attached to you. Of course you could be mean to everyone else: his mother, his friends, his dog. He is protective of everyone he loves and is super in touch with their vulnerabilities, so if you bully "the weak," he will surely come to their defense and give you hell.

Of course if you want to end your affair on a nice note, you could do that in a couple of ways. The more simple and honest way is to tell him that it's over, that your decision is final, but that he will always have an ally and friend in you . . . and mean it, sweetie. Keep up the "platonic" boundaries, though, because he has no problem sleeping with and falling in love with his friends and misconstruing this as a "relationship."

The other thing you could do is to write him a long romantic letter and leave it behind, after you take all your things to leave town. Include lots of sentiments that make absolutely no sense like "It is my great love for you that has inspired me to explore my own ability to love, in another place, at another time." Mr. Pisces has such a convoluted psyche that all this will probably seem completely logical to him. And he'll always keep a candle burning for you. Just be careful, though, since he does practice the art of magic and the art of stalking. And he's superpsychic, sweetie: he *will* find you.

The Three Faces of Pisces

Every sign is broken up into three decanates, each of which gives the Sun sign a distinctive flavor. Keep in mind, though, that the Sun enters and leaves each sign a day later or earlier during different years. Make the proper adjustments for boys born on the cusp of their sign. Wipe that dumb look off your face and just do it. All right, you Pisces boys, no whining, just check an ephemeris and see what the exact dates of your (or your pal's) Sun sign were for the year in question, divide by three, and there you will find the correct decanates.

First-Decanate Pisces (February 19–29): The Neptune Decanate

Early Pisces men are the most Piscean of the bunch. They have a hard time being practical and are often very dreamy and unrealistic. They are extremely psychic, and often their strong intuition makes them even more scared of the real world. Art or healing is their true calling and their true salvation. By acting as a vehicle for the "muses" to come through them (acting, painting, writing, etc.) or by focusing their supreme sensitivities on those who need them (healing), they can make their own fractured psyches whole again.

Second-Decanate Pisces (March 1–10): The Lunar Decanate

These boys are the most home loving of the Pisces group. They are attached to their families and are great nurturers. They love to eat and they usually love to cook, too. They are gentle and protective of their loved ones, but can also be extremely moody. The lunar influence of Cancer makes them more susceptible to the emotional moodswings associated with the moon's frequent transits. Water is literally healing for them, and they should be near it and in it as often as possible (while sober of course). These Pisceans will find it the easiest to make a home and a life with a lover. They crave stability and usually know how to find it.

Third-Decanate Pisces (March 11–20): The Pluto Decanate

Third-decanate Pisces men are sexy and dramatic and are drawn to the dark side of life. They know that they can see God and the devil simultaneously when they are having great sex. That's why sex is such a drug to them. These men possess great powers that can be used for self-destruction or for self-transformation. They're the hell-and-back types, which is why they tend to be such closeted geniuses. They need to go through many dark nights of the soul before they can look at themselves in the mirror and say, "I love you." Once they conquer the challenge of self-love, they make wonderful, passionate, and exciting lovers with surprising staying power.

If You Have His Chart

A copy of his chart will tell you in a lot more detail what Mr. Pisces is really like. If he has a lot of Sagittarius in his chart, he is a great philosopher but may have the most difficulty really understanding himself. Scorpio moon or rising makes him even more sexy and mysterious. Lots of Taurus or Capricorn in his chart makes him more practical and reliable than the average Fish. A Leo moon makes him a great performer and a true hedonist.

Two

Compatibility

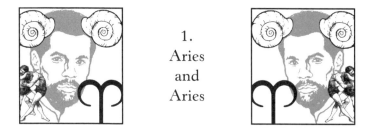

1.
Aries
and
Aries

What do these two have in common? "Everything," you might answer, but in fact, they are completely different. You see, every Aries has a desire to stand out from the crowd and express his individuality in a strong, unmistakable way. So when an Aries man meets another Aries man, it could go a few different ways. There could be the requisite "Who's got a bigger dick?" contest (literally, figuratively, or both). Both of these fellows probably are rather competitive and would need to figure out who's in charge pretty early on.

When dating, these two gentlemen (and I use the term loosely) could find each other ever so exciting. Both have boundless energy and will seek out excitement and thrills like nobody's business. The more active they are, the better. Boredom is something neither can tolerate, but if they are left to their own devices too much, they might start to drive each other crazy. Imagine two little boys playing together. It's fun at first, but then they just want to fight when they've exhausted all the possibilities of things to do: cowboys and Indians, war, rim jobs . . .

You see, what can be missing between these two guys is imagination. They may both have primal reactions to each other, which is why sex can be so rough and good. But it may be hard for them to communicate in a form other than the ones animals use.

If both Aries dudes are evolved (or take this relationship as a starting point for evolving together), there is tremendous potential. That means that when one of them is feeling like expressing himself in a new way, or trying something new within the relationship, the other one encourages him, rather than beating his spirit down and dominating him, or just saying, "Shut up and take off your pants."

Sex is the ingredient that pulls them together, but it's like candy
. . . you can't live on it.

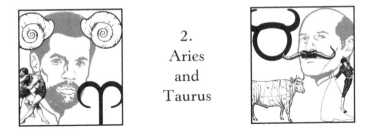

2.
Aries
and
Taurus

These guys are each so strong in their own right that I think they
would make quite an impressive (and intimidating) duo. Whereas
the Aries man has a type of toughness that is apparent right away,
the Taurus man is more subtle. Remember, their astrological rulers
are opposites. Aries is ruled by Mars, and Taurus is ruled by Venus.
The Aries man is drawn to action, and fighting, while the more
mellow Taurus man loves life to be serene and quiet.

Even though these guys are so different, there is a sexy chemistry
between them, which can carry over from the bedroom (or the
pickup truck) into the rest of their lives together. Because each possesses so much inner strength (Aries in the form of bravery, Taurus
in the form of an iron will), they are able to hold their own with
each other, and that gives each darling gay boy a certain sense of
divine security with the other. Neither has to worry that the other
is too fragile or is going to fall apart when things get rough or when
conflicts arise.

The main challenge for the Aries man with the Taurus man is
that the Ram is likely to crave conflict and excitement daily, while
the Taurus is a sucker for stability. If they are able to complement
each other—the Aries could encourage the Taurus to stop eating
like a pig in front of the TV for hours on end and support Mr.
Taurus's secret musical ambitions; the Taurus could help the Aries
to stop starting new projects that never go anywhere and could teach
Mr. Aries to see his dreams through to the end—then they could
be quite good for each other.

And when it comes to sex, this could certainly be a hot pairing.

Mr. Fast (Aries) in bed with Mr. Slow (Taurus) could just add up to nights together that are just soooo right.

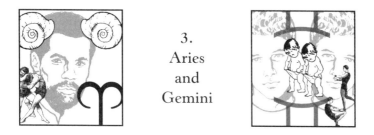

3.
Aries
and
Gemini

This couple has a great deal of potential together. Their signs are sextile and make a smooth and easy angle to each other, so they are apt to rub each other the right away, from the beginning. Surprisingly, though, they may not get to the rubbing part immediately because the Gemini man may want to test the wit and cleverness of the Aries man. The Gemini is constantly in search of entertainment and intellectual challenges. I don't care if he's a complete disco slut who reads only porn magazines (in which case I guarantee you he *does* read the articles), he still needs to use his brain, much more than the Aries man, who prefers to just use his dick.

The Aries man, however, will certainly be turned on by the Gemini's sexy and alluring ways. He knows that he will have to come back with many witty retorts and surprising verbal observations to pass the Gemini's requisite IQ test. But the Aries man also knows that man (or queen) cannot live by bitchy comeback alone. He senses that the Gemini would love to be physically and sexually overpowered by someone who is unimpressed by verbal foreplay. And he's right. Basically, these men are playing a game, and it's a fun one.

But after their first night together, what then? Well, the Gemini man is intensely people-oriented and will probably pull the Aries man out of his loner mode and into a ready-made social life, which the Gemini has created. The Gemini will enjoy showing off this real man, but will also enjoy watching the Aries hold his own. He ain't afraid of nobody, and certainly not his Gemini partner. And the Gemini man loves being "sassy" in public and getting punished in private as a bad boy. On that level, they were made for each other.

It's on a communication level, when arguments arise, that they will each have to work on being more sensitive to the other. The Gemini man is smart, clever, and always has the right words to say . . . but where is his heart? He must remember to nurture the relationship, and not just to win the petty battles. The Aries man is honest and can be brutal, which adds up to a type of brutal honesty that some would find unduly cruel. He needs to lighten up a little and stop trying to shut the Gemini up by intimidating him.

They both need to realize that they share the same worst fear: neither can bear the idea of being immobilized, both live for *movement*. The Gemini needs to be moving forward in the mental sense (his curiosity is insatiable), and the Aries needs to be moving forward in an action-oriented way. If they can keep in mind that they both need to and *want* to constantly progress, I think these homos could make quite the happy, humpy couple.

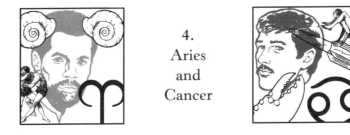

**4.
Aries
and
Cancer**

Both these guys are just big babies at heart. The Aries man is the kind who screams and bangs his fists (or perhaps just bangs *and* fists) to get what he wants *now!* The Cancer man sulks if he does not get the complete coddling he needs half the time and the total privacy he needs the other half of the time. I don't know if anyone can tolerate them together . . . except for each other.

Aries is such a daddy and Cancer such a mommy that together their relationship almost seems—dare I say it—downright heterosexual! Unlike their more inhibited straight counterparts, these boys can reach new levels of pleasure by role-playing like crazy. The S/M side of their natures really needs to be explored.

This is a relationship about teaching and learning, though, so they can't simply do what comes easiest. Sure the Cancer is capable of complete submission and the Aries just loves to pull the "If you don't stop crying, I'll *really* give you something to cry about" routine, but it's when they do a little role reversal that the level of their passion and *trust* really comes out.

Their sex life is ultimately a bizarre mystery . . . a twisted prison drama. And ultimately it should be kept completely secret from the rest of the world. But if they can reveal their secret longings and shame to each other, in bed, they will be bonded together forever.

If either refuses to work through his own repression (and believe me, sweetie, they each possess major complexes and conflicts regarding their parents), then the relationship really won't go far. But if both are brave and can dive in sex first, they may find true love, as well as true satisfaction.

Sounds extreme, doesn't it? What about just the "dating" part of their relationship? Forget it. These guys will either go from zero to ninety miles per hour in the first month or will be so annoyed by one another that they never speak again.

Keep in mind, too, that this is a fire (Aries) and water (Cancer) liaison. If they are open to the other's differences, this could be a delicious steam bath, but if the timing or the other planets in their respective charts are too conflicted, it will be over before it starts.

If they are compatible on a level deeper than their Sun signs, then the main thing they can teach each other is how to understand their own subconscious minds, and to stop acting out as a baby would have to because a baby doesn't have the ability to take care of himself.

If the bond is a strong one, though . . . oh, *baby!*

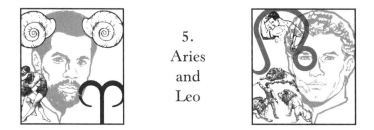

**5.
Aries
and
Leo**

These two will hit it off like gangbusters right away, in most instances. Both are fire signs, which means they love the nightlife and have got to boogie. And their enthusiasm for life combined could provide enough energy to light up all the neon signs on Broadway, sweetie. The Aries man will probably come after the Leo first. He loves to woo and conquer, which is fine by the Leo, who is generally too proud to chase but adores being adored. Both men are warm and expressive and see no reason to hold back their feelings and their affections.

In bed, these guys are likely to be simply blown away by their mutual fabulousness! In fact, they may drive their friends crazy by *bragging* about how great their sex life is . . . much to the nausea of said friends. But their sex life will be great, in most cases because there is a core compatibility between them. The Leo, however, might be a little bit more uptight or rigid in his repertoire than the Aries. And the Leo will not appreciate it if the Aries mocks him or tries to push him too hard to get into a rough-trade kind of scene with him.

The Aries must be careful not to look elsewhere for the kind of sleazy experience he desires. It will be the ram's loss if he puts the Leo on the same kind of pedestal straight men of another era put their wives on. The Leo man will not stand for a relationship that is not monogamous (unless he has some serious Gemini, Sagittarius, or Aquarius influence in his chart), so the Aries had better figure out how to treat the Leo like a prostitute at night and still hold hands with him in public by day.

The Leo man should be open about the fact that although he was instantly attracted to the Aries, he still needs time to feel the kind of trust that comes with a committed relationship. The Aries needs to grow the hell up and develop some patience. He will be glad he did when he finds that his own bedroom (shared with Mr. Leo) has turned into the divine dungeon of his dreams. It just may not happen overnight, boys. But it definitely can happen.

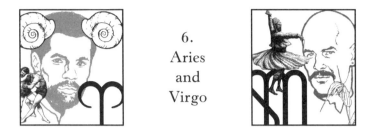

6.
Aries
and
Virgo

The main thing these two boys have in common is their sick, immoral, and absolutely orgasmic fixation with the bathroom. The Virgo man, of course, is known for his cleanliness, or his inner guilt at being so decidedly *unclean*. The clean types do really insist on a sparkling bowl and completely hair-free sink. The messy Virgo rebels against his inner need for order and *godliness* by acting as if his mother is around to pick up after him all the time. Aries men, however, come in only one flavor: they are all anally fixated and find bathrooms (especially public toilets . . . how unusual for a gay man!) to be huge turn-ons.

The potential for various scenes is infinite. The Aries man simply loves to destroy the bathroom with his manly messes, and the Virgo man can barely contain his passion when he is forced to clean it all up with his toothbrush or tongue. On this base level, it's a match made in heaven.

Now what about in the rest of their relationship? Well, when they are not praying to the porcelain god, these guys live for something else: work. The Aries man is as driven as they come. When he has a goal in mind, he is a well of boundless energy and will stop at nothing to get it done . . . although, he is a little less effective when it comes to *long*-term goals. The Virgo man is more interested in work itself rather than the outcome and either is a workaholic himself or wants one as his lover. So these two guys do have some common ground.

However, Aries and Virgo is an odd combination, and if these two like each other at all, it will be a surprise to many of their closest friends. But you can't judge these two books by their covers (if you did, you would think the Aries man was obsessed with porn and the Virgo man with pre-Victorian novels). It's their deeper motivations that will hold them together . . . the substance of who they are as individuals, and as a couple, not the style. Because, honey, their styles couldn't be more contrary.

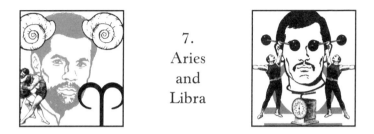

7.
Aries
and
Libra

This is a case of opposites who could either attract or repel. The Mars-ruled Aries man is direct, straightforward, and totally devoid of tact. The Venus-ruled Libra man is diplomatic, soft-spoken, and a compulsive liar. All right, that's the most extreme picture. But these boys do bring out the extremes in one another.

The Aries man is likely to be charmed by the Libra man's soft and subtle ways. The Libra man has an air of refinement that the Aries finds rather enticing. The Aries loves to have his . . . er . . . *ego* stroked, and that is the Libra man's specialty. Mr. Libra, however, can have a bit of an icy reserve at times. Those who know him best have hurt him in the past by accusing him of being too cold, removed, or cerebral. The forthright honesty of the Aries man can encourage Mr. Libra to be more open and warm, too. They each have a fantastic effect on the other's popularity. And popularity is important to both of them in deep and primal ways. The Aries man desperately needs to feel liked, and the Libra man hates to be alone.

The friends of Mr. Aries will comment, after he's being dating a Libra for a while, that he has "mellowed" and moved up the food chain. The Libra's pals will tell him that his relationship with the Aries man has made him more passionate and approachable. They really can bring out the best in each other.

And when it comes to their sexual relationship, these boys can fit perfectly together. The Aries seems the obvious top and the Libra the obvious bottom, but it doesn't have to be that way (especially if the Libra has lots of Sagittarius in his chart and the Aries has a lot of Pisces). But however they set up their respective roles, the roles will probably stick. This is a question of "do the parts fit together or not?" If the chemistry isn't there in the bedroom, then so be it. The relationship will fizzle quickly enough. But if it is there, these two can be quite a winning team.

If they pass the initial three-month test and decide that this is a "keeper," then they should be aware of some of the long-term challenges. Because they were born under opposite signs, they must realize that at times the ever-moving planets will affect them in opposite ways. During their birthday seasons especially (early spring and early autumn), they could find that when one is up and having a grand old time skating through life, the other is feeling oppressed and depressed.

If they are loving enough (and observant enough of the cycles of astrology and the cycles in their relationship), they can be strong for each other, and sensitive to each other's moods the whole year round.

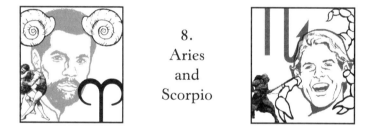

8.
Aries
and
Scorpio

These two men make quite a dynamic duo. Both are charismatic, forceful, and action-oriented. Although Scorpio is a water sign, it is known as the most fiery of water signs and therefore already has a lot in common with fiery Aries. Another thing they have in common is the fiery red planet, Mars. Mars, the planet that symbolizes action, passion, and the sexual oomph that puts the passion in a love relationship, is the ruling planet of Aries and the coruler (playing second banana to the other planet that is associated with war) of Scorpio.

As a team, these two can be like great allies in a war. We're talking superpowers, baby. When they have a common goal, they can go forward and fight harder than any other pairing to achieve what they've set out to. But here's the rub: neither of them is good at just enjoying peacetime. Both are uncomfortable with contentment, and this could be a problem if they don't come up with a positive outlet for their fighting spirits.

Basically, they have to psych themselves out and keep moving the finish line, so that they are always moving forward to face some big macho challenge, sometimes separately and sometimes together.

Both of these guys are directors who want to run the show. It is probably best if they have separate assignments in life so that they do not totally compete with each other.

In the sexual arena, that fire that I spoke of earlier will certainly come in handy regularly. The Scorpio likes the Aries's approach to sex: that it shall be totally and completely consuming and over-whelming. The Aries is aroused and sometimes frightened by the Scorpio's sexual dance with the dark side . . . and no one loves to face up to his fears more than Mr. Aries.

Whether it's in bed or out, though, these two guys must con-stantly remind themselves and each other to talk, talk, and talk some more. They are both so action-oriented and possess such startling tunnel vision that they must really work on the day-to-day main-tenance of their union. "Fuck me" and "Go fuck yourself" just won't cut it, boys. Try learning a new language, together.

9.
Aries
and
Sagittarius

These two fire signs are naturally compatible and will probably hit it off right from the start. Both of these guys are intensely *physical*. They are athletic, energetic, and youthful . . . so youthful that both often get described as "immature" (behind their backs, of course). Both men are also quite oblivious to criticism because their egos are so strong and their bodies so active (they're both out running to face the next race and don't have the time to let anything negative stick to them). The main thing they have in common, and which they can help to bring out even more with each other, is a big, brave form of optimism. They are doers who believe that anything is possible. If someone says to the Sag man, "Bet you can't win an Olympic medal in pole-vaulting," the very next day you will find him out on the track with a big stick (at least I think it was a stick); or more likely, if a fellow barfly tells Mr. Sag, "Betcha can't down that pitcher of beer in under thirty seconds," by gum he'll pull out a watch with a second hand and start guzzling before you can say "Drunken whore." And the Aries man also believes in the world and, even more, in himself. If a friend tells the Aries guy, "I don't know if you and Mr. Sag can go beyond just fucking to have a real relationship," he will start right then and there to prove that this cynical friend is wrong.

The quandary faced by the Aries man and the Sagittarius man who are interested in each other comes down to a simple question: Who is going to chase whom? Now this is the kind of bet that could really make a lot of money for a smart bookie. At gunpoint, I would have to put my money on the Sag chasing the Aries. The Aries is more independent and can go his own way more easily. Once the hunter-esque Sag (dig that bow and arrow in the Archer's arms) gets a bee in his bonnet, he won't rest until he captures the game.

Once these two are "an item," they've got a good shot at happiness. They both enjoy similar activities and share many of the same views of life. The real secret is keeping this relationship a passionate, romantically connected one. There is the possibility that their coupling is so "easy" that they simply drift into a nice friendship.

These two might meet young, go out, break up, and then get back together years later. If both are mature and have lived a little, they can make their relationship last a long time, if they really make a commitment. Both want to live with a high standard of integrity, and each can inspire the other to do so.

10.
Aries
and
Capricorn

The main thing these darling gents have in common can be summed up in one word: *ambition*. For Mr. Capricorn, that is his key word. He views life (and relationships) in a most linear way. He cautiously but tenaciously moves forward always with a goal in mind. He usually gets what he wants—after a long and painstaking process (oh, yes, he is quite the masochist)—and usually what he wants is some kind of *power*. Mr. Aries, on the other hand, rarely looks beyond the short term. He sets a goal for himself and takes the quickest and most aggressive route.

These two men will undoubtedly respect each other. They both have strong belief systems and may find the philosophy of the other quite fascinating, and disturbing. Their Sun signs make a hard angle to each other, so probably there will have to be soft, easy aspects within their charts to balance out the surface tension.

Work will either bring them together or help them to stay together. Upon first meeting, they could be strongly turned off by each other. Or the Aries could say something so blunt and crushing that he horrifies the Capricorn. Or the Capricorn could be so stoic and standoffish that the Ram will be sure that the Goat hates him.

Strong negative reactions can sometimes foreshadow great passion, which could certainly be true in the case of these boys. Once they do get down and dirty, their sex life could be a real mystery . . . certainly to people who know them both well, who may simply respond, "Huh?" . . . but it could be a real mystery to them, too.

The Aries man will find the Capricorn man quick, mysterious, and enigmatic. Capricorn won't give it away easily—meaning his body or his soul—even when he's on all fours screaming, "Daddy." Yes, even in that tender moment, the Aries fellow knows that his

Capricorn boyfriend is holding something back. Naturally, this inspires the Ram to ram his way in even harder to find out what this Goat really wants.

The Capricorn will find himself surprised by a real and passionate *yearning* for his Aries lover. He will find the Aries man so real, and so forceful, that he is actually comforted by the Ram's seeming roughness. If you smell a heavy S/M potential here, naturally you couldn't be more right.

When the lights and the clothes are on, that is when the real challenge comes in. Both men can bring out a type of cruelty in the other, and they really need to watch this. Mr. Aries, here's a tip: try taking a softer approach when your prone-to-depression Capricorn boyfriend is in a blue mood. Talk to him and support him unconditionally . . . don't just tell him to "snap out of it." It's called sensitivity, you idiot. And Mr. Capricorn, try not to let your own Saturnian negativity burst the bubble of your ever optimistic Aries boyfriend. Yes, you are the old soul and he the young one in this relationship, but maybe you can learn something from this "kid," you jaded queen you.

Once a bond is formed between these two men, the loving will be easy. It's the way they fight that will determine whether they stay together forever or part, disgusted with each other.

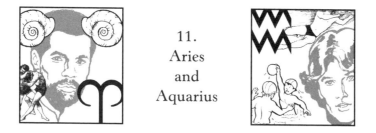

**11.
Aries
and
Aquarius**

The main thing these two men have in common is a fierce sense of individuality and a desire for independence and freedom. Aries the fire sign and Aquarius the air sign are generally compatible, and both possess a code of integrity that overlaps a great deal. The Aries man believes in doing what he sets out to in the world, not just talking about it. And the Aquarius, too, believes that the future is determined by what we do today. Both share a love affair with the future and probably share the guilty pleasure of enjoying the cheesiest science fiction that pop culture has to offer.

In bed, you can expect more cheese. They like to take the most clichéd role-playing games (many of which you may have read about in this very book!) and add a little twist. The Aquarius man is the true original thinker in the zodiac and will just love testing out some of his cold, textbook theories about sex and fetishes, by using himself and his Aries lover as the guinea pigs. In fact, neighbors may hear the Aries man scream, "Squeal like a piggie!" The Aries isn't known for taking the most imaginative routes in bed, but he will relish the chance to wear some new hats with his Aquarius beau. The Aquarius will appreciate the fiery sex drive of the Aries. After all, the Aquarius realizes, when left to his own devices, he can be a bit of a robot. These boys really can bring out the best in each other.

Yet there is a feeling, even among Aries/Aquarius gay male couples who've been together for years, that their relationship is still a divine experiment. Monogamy is a definite question mark. Both probably need to slip off and get off with other people from time to time. The Aries might not go for a truly "open" relationship, though. And deception is not something that makes either of them feel good. So what's the answer, dear readers?

That's right: threesomes, and plenty of 'em. Aquarius, more than any sign, loves the group scene, and Aries is happy to be worshiped by two (or more) rather than one. This predilection could be the glue that holds them together for years to come. Theirs is a wild experiment, but it just might work.

**12.
Aries
and
Pisces**

Although these guys are very different, Aries being a blunt fire sign and Pisces being a subtle water sign, they may actually have a lot in common. Because their birthdays are usually so close together, there is a strong likelihood that some of their personal planets, such as Venus and Mercury, could fall in the other's sign. For example, an Aries with Venus in Pisces is likely to have a strong psychic bond to his Pisces lover (he is probably also a lot more giving and empathetic than your garden-variety Aries).

These guys are like two unusual tastes that can often go great together. The Aries will usually be immediately protective of the more sensitive Pisces. And the Pisces man is not above exploiting that dynamic. Oh, calm down, you crazy queen, I'm not saying that's a *bad* thing. The Pisces just knows instinctively that in this case the means justify the ends. So if the Aries feels more manly because he is protecting the gentle, vulnerable Pisces, what's so terrible? Although, lovable as they are, most Pisceans are great manipulators, it ain't as cut-and-dry as all that. Remember, Pisces is ruled by trippy Neptune, the planet of healing and illusion. It's mind over matter, really. And in this case, the Pisces is just quietly training the Aries to *actually be* his protector, which is the role that Aries really wants to fulfill anyway. Just 'cause neither one is admitting it doesn't make it wrong. And besides, that's the premise that all those 1950s sitcoms were based on anyway. It's called "the hunter gets captured by the game," sweetie.

But how can this union last over the years, as opposed to all those real-life 1950s hetero unions that mostly ended in divorce? Well, let's start in the privacy of their own home. Mr. Pisces on some level knows that he has been a bad boy by setting his Aries man up, without letting him in on his little plot. That's why it's such a relief and a thrill to both of them when Mr. Aries takes charge of the household and gives his bad little Pisces the hard spanking he deserves and desires. Part of the role of the protector is to discipline, too, and they both know that.

But can regular spankings keep a relationship going through the years? Well, in this case, probably, but here are a few other things these two gentlemen need to keep in mind. Two words, one concept: giving and receiving. The Aries has earned an unfair reputation as "selfish," when really he is just honest about wanting pleasure. So, yes, during the first year, they will both get off on how much, say, Mr. Pisces enjoys blowing Mr. Aries and how much Mr. Aries enjoys getting blown. But Mr. Aries wants to give, too! And I'm just using sex as an example . . . these boys are the princes of acting out their emotional relationship in bed. So Mr. Pisces must learn to stop manipulating (yes, this time I mean manipulating, and nothing else) and to trust that his Aries man really wants to give to him, and let him. Mr. Aries, on the other hand, needs to really learn the art of giving and give the Pisces what he wants, not just what the Aries would want if he was going to "get" something. For instance, Aries . . . try buying your Pisces lover the silk underwear he wants, not the leather chaps you think he'd looked so doable in.

These two, if they really look beyond the surface, can understand each other on a deep, deep level. And in doing so they will both learn to understand themselves better, warts and all.

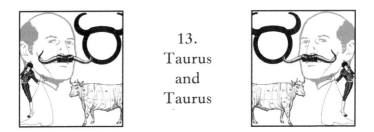

13.
Taurus
and
Taurus

This is a definite hit-or-miss pairing. Getting started could be the hardest part for these slow-moving men. Taurus is known as the most patient sign in the zodiac, so it might take several years just for them to get to a first date. When they do get together, they will probably be quite pleasantly surprised by how compatible they are in the sack. Tauruses tend to be ultrasensual and are greatly affected by their environment. Although a Taurus man may act too butch (at first) to care about good music, nice incense, and sheets made of some luxurious material, in his heart he is really turned on by all those extras. When both boys realize that the other digs the same sexy, delicious scene as he does, there will be much cause for celebration.

Both attach easily, and once they develop a routine together, they will probably stay together out of habit and comfort more than anything else. Which does not mean that there is no romantic potential.

They have so much in common and will probably feel a real sense of kinship with each other.

The main challenge these two diamonds in the rough could experience is putting up with the other's stubbornness and inflexibility. One Taurus on his own could be an immovable object, but with two together, we are talking rock hard and rigid as you could imagine, and I don't mean in the obvious sense, darling.

These two queens may need a referee, but both are too set in their ways to even admit that there's a problem. Hopefully one or both of them has enough mutable (adaptable) or cardinal (action-oriented) signs in their charts to mellow out that fixed Taurus energy.

The way for this relationship to last though, is if both will agree to give in once in a while. Perhaps they can come to an agreement like this. Every time one gives in a little, the other Taurus has to give him the sexual favor of his choice. Ah, the games these boys must play.

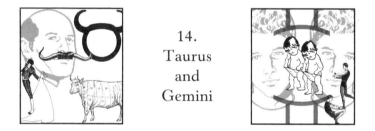

14.
Taurus
and
Gemini

These boys are an odd but definitely cute combination. Chances are, if they are drawn to each other, either the Gemini has a good bit of Taurus in his chart, or the Gemini has an earthy clump of Taurus in his. The initial secret to this pair's attraction can be summed up by the old-girl group anthem "It's in His Kiss." The Taurus gay man is intensely sensual, and although he likes to get down to business, he loves to explore with his lips and tongue. The Gemini fella also loves to use his mouth (he is the sign least likely to shut up!), and together these two can turn making out into an art form.

After they've made their friends sick by sucking face in restaurants (how can anyone else eat? I ask you), they may find that they really are two different animals. This is a pairing that tends to be exotic because these guys do generally have vastly different styles.

The most obvious one is this: the Taurus man is usually quiet (except after he's had a bottle of wine and feels the need to pontif- icate for hours, in a sleep-inducing monotone), while the Gemini guy is a real chatterbox. Mr. Gemini is a social butterfly who loves to talk with a variety of people, every day, all the time, while Mr. Taurus prefers to get to know people slowly. In fact, Mr. Taurus usually has a close inner circle, and most of those people sought him out. Mr. Gemini is a social whore. Whoever can entertain him he will go to.

Mr. Gemini also needs lots of stimulation in other ways. He is full of nervous energy. He likes to read, dance, draw, make love . . . usually all at the same time. Mr. Taurus prefers to focus on one thing and is perfectly able to entertain himself.

What the future holds for this couple will depend a lot on the other factors in their charts. In general, though, I think they could have a good relationship if the Gemini learns to focus and live life on a deeper level. Who better to show him the way than Mr. Tau- rus. And the Bull can in turn learn to lighten up and have more fun and break out of his blessed routines, if he takes a page from the Gemini's book.

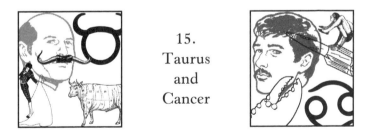

15.
Taurus
and
Cancer

This is a terribly sweet combination, one that is likely to work for- ever. I think I'm going to be sick. Both the Taurus man and the Cancer man are major homebodies, who can make quite a cozy little "lesbian style" nest together. Of course, they are *not* lesbians, so they are required, as gay men, to put up track lighting and make their home look as if it's out of the pages of a magazine (and I don't mean *Boy's Life*).

Once together, these boys will get into a groove almost right away, but the getting together could take a little work. First of all, both boys expect the other to come to him. If push comes to shove, I bet it will be the Cancer who makes the first move. The Crab is after all a cardinal sign, which represents leadership. Of course he is also the moodiest man in the zodiac, so it will all depend on the mood he is in at the time. If these two stability-minded men don't meet across a crowded room, they are likely to be introduced by friends or family members. Both have small but loyal allies who surround them at all times.

And the pal or cousin who introduces them is probably a smart cookie, because these two do really have so much in common. Both love good food (and come from the "food is love" school) and are probably great cooks, too. They are both slightly on the conventional side, meaning their values are pretty down-to-earth. They think a good home, a good job, and money in the bank are all important. When they are young, they might like to party, but that won't last forever, believe me.

The main challenge to this duo is that they are both so into security, and *hibernating*, that neither may push the other to grow or evolve. And as those of us who've been around the block know, the more things stay the same, the more likely they are to go no-where fast. And that's how these two could end up getting a D-I-V-O-R-C-E.

Now if the goal is to stay together, there is one important thing they must remember above all else, and that's this: *don't withdraw*. Both men have a tendency to pull inward and say too little rather than too much when he is upset. And both are also likely to put "keeping the peace" above communicating, which in a relationship can be deadly. Luckily, both these fellows have a wry sense of humor and are tremendously affectionate. When times are tough, those are the traits they must cling to, to keep them going.

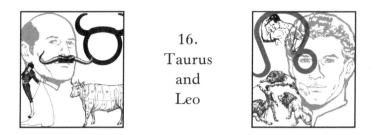

16.
Taurus
and
Leo

This combination can best be described with one word: *luxurious.* Both the Taurus man and the Leo man are greedy on the inside when it comes to their deep desire for a rich lifestyle. If you think these guys can be happy for long living in a cold-water flat, with barely enough money for a box of noodles, you must be crazy. These boys bring out the materialistic in each other, and chances are they can get to the top together.

But first, they have to *get* together, and how does that happen, you ask? The Taurus will probably gravitate toward the Leo and give the Lion king (or queen, whatever) the praise and attention he craves so deeply. Both men will sense (and rightly so) that the other is loyal and grounded. Each of them is what we call a fixed sign, which means that they are stubborn, able to stay on one course, and definitely *not* great lovers of change.

These two men definitely have a similar emotional makeup. Each of them is loyal, strong, proud, and hates to ask for help. Both also like to make life as simple as possible. For the Taurus that means making his social life revolve around his home or his office (he hates to go out of his way), and for the Leo that means getting a maid.

Where these boys differ is in their energy level and the ways they express themselves to the world. The Leo is the diva of the house and needs an exhausting amount of attention and adulation at all times. The Leo man needs an audience and a fan club, and once the initial blush of romance dies down, the Taurus may find this just a tad annoying. The Taurus likes his peace and quiet, to such an extent that the Leo may find him to be a crashing bore after a while.

If these two have enough other planets in their charts that are compatible, they will probably find each other's differences endearing rather than annoying. If one of them has a Pisces moon or rising sign and the other has Virgo moon or ascendant, their chemistry should be especially good. The main way for this relationship to work, though, is for them to get rich and get rich quick. They both make great Princes and horrific paupers.

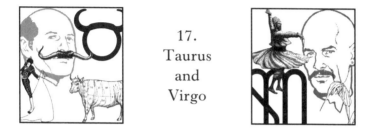

17.
Taurus
and
Virgo

These two earth signs are, generally, very compatible. They both value work and stability and tend to prefer concrete answers in life, not elusive mysteries. Both are practical and possess a pragmatic attitude about sex (although the Taurus man is more of a romantic than he initially lets on). These boys just groove well together, on the dance floor and between the sheets.

The Taurus man is usually drawn to the Virgo man's tight body and quick mind, while the Virgo man is incredibly attracted to the Taurus's manly yet refined style. When these two come together in bed (and they will, again and again and again), it will feel *mighty real* for both of them. These men will realize why they are made of flesh and blood to begin with . . . to feel passion like this.

Once they start dating, they will probably get serious rather quickly. Each might feel that he's found the guy he's been waiting for. And, depending on their other planets, they could be quite right. Their main challenge will be to overcome their innate practicality and keep the romance alive in their relationship.

Naturally, this task begins and ends in the bedroom (kitchen, dungeon, wherever they like to do it). The Virgo man should remember not to think of sex as just a practical function (so that he can get off and go back to his precious work), but as a real way to connect with his Taurus loverboy. And as gruff and blasé as Mr.

Taurus may seem on the outside, he secretly desires nights, and days and nights, of pure unadulterated pleasure. So, Mr. Virgo, take your time, please, and use your imagination.

The Taurus man should also find out what his Virgo lover's fantasies are. Oh, forget the ones he's told you. He's got more . . . and they are all *very* specific. Luckily, the Taurus man is unflappable and unshockable, so the Virgo man should be able to get over his inhibitions quickly with his Taurus boyfriend.

Both these guys are good long-term bets for each other as long as they keep those home fires burning.

18.
Taurus
and
Libra

Both these men are ruled by Venus, the planet of love, and together they make quite the romantic pair. They both have a strong sense of aesthetic beauty, and each is extremely sensitive to his environment. Mr. Libra is more affected by the way things look. He needs everything to be *pretty* or he gets upset. Mr. Taurus is more ruled by feel. He likes sensually pleasing fabric to touch his skin and is repulsed by all things plastic (including credit cards . . . he resents finance charges like you wouldn't believe).

Chances are good that they will be brought together through art or that the arts will keep them together. If they are both the artistic kind, they may feel as if they have found a kindred spirit in the other. The Taurus is imaginative and instinctual, and if he is, say, a musician or a designer, he is probably able to tap into his own talent and vision in a feeling-oriented way. He is not usually one to analyze. He just does it. The Libra man is much more intellectual and loves to weigh both sides of everything, sometimes to the frustration of the get-to-the-point Taurus. If the Libra man is a painter, let's say, or an actor, he will love doing his art as much as he loves talking about it and figuring out where his God-given gifts come from (yes, the *pretty* boy is vain!). Even though their approaches are different, the basic things that turn them on are the same.

Both also love being in a relationship. The Libra man can't live without one, and the Taurus man knows he can live much better when he's in one. And sexually, this a rather unusual but fascinating pairing. The Libra man likes to be dominated by his Taurus lover. He likes the Taurus's rough-and-tumble, real-man ways, which make the Libra feel more like a little schoolgirl. You can imagine what fodder there is for fantasy between these boys.

Once the postcoital cigarette has been smoked (the Taurus actually prefers a cigar), what then? How do these boys make a life together in the long run? Well, as I said in the beginning, artistic endeavors are extremely inspiring to both, so even if they don't work as artists (or especially if they do), they will both find that their love deepens when they see and experience works of art together. Whether it's the opera or the movies, these fellows will find common ground talking and often arguing, in a fun way, about how they see the world, and what is "beautiful" and what is "ugly." It's called the search for truth, which is what all art is about, right?

19.
Taurus
and
Scorpio

Here we have another example, like Aries and Libra, of opposites either attracting or repelling each other. With these two, I strongly suspect, there is a great, great chance for attraction. Both men are mysterious in different ways, and strong, strong, strong! Already, you can tell, this is going to be a battle of wills. In the beginning, they are likely to find each other's differing opinions endearing. That will wear off soon enough, but the sexual attraction is likely to last a long, long time.

The Scorpio man has a more serious approach to sex. He is drawn to the dark and mystical and may open up a whole new world to the Taurus man. Mr. Taurus may be frightened by the world of sexual heights and emotional depths that the Scorpio drags him into. It will really depend on the Taurus man's planets in this case (he being the more immovable object of the two). If the Taurus man has planets that make him yearn for intensity and excitement more than the average Bull, this could be a lasting union. If not, the Taurus may walk away and leave the Scorpio a bit brokenhearted.

Both men have a similar lesson to learn from this relationship. It's all about protection. Each is extremely self-protective and must learn to let his guard down with the other and actually trust a little. Oddly, both will probably have an immediate "I trust you! I don't trust you! My mother! My sister!" reaction to the other, upon first meeting, like Faye Dunaway in *Chinatown*. This relationship is a most primal one. Logic will have no place here, honey! So, I guess you could say these boys will end up lovers or enemies.

To be lovers, in every sense of the word, these guys need to slay some inner demons. First off, this is one relationship that better be monogamous. Neither of these guys has a "whatever" attitude about fidelity. Maybe it was different back in the past, when the Scorpio was dating a wild Sagittarius, or when the Taurus was banging an Aquarius, as a divine experiment. But now that they are together, the rules are different, and these rules were *not* meant to be broken, *under any circumstances.*

Still, security and fidelity alone do not a marriage make. (I know, I know, I know, you're just dating . . . but I'm telling you this is all or nothing, baby.) These boys need to learn to express their anger at each other and not hold things inside, and it helps if they have the same goals in life, too. If they do, they are likely to grow together instead of apart.

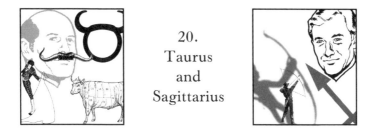

20.
Taurus
and
Sagittarius

The word that comes to mind for this duo is dirty. Taurus is an earth sign and is the earthiest of the three (beating out Virgo and Capricorn), and Sagittarius is the earthiest of all fire signs. Together these boys make quite a nasty pair. If there is an attraction between them, chances are they will get together quickly. There is no need for subtlety here. Both men are drawn to extremes when it comes to food and sex. They both tend to overindulge and then go through long bouts of abstinence.

Most of their friends will probably be happy to see them together and could easily give this relationship a stamp of approval. That's because they can finally stop complaining about how horny they are and actually indulge their libidos with a partner who is just as sex-obsessed and disgusting as they are.

So what's the challenge here? Well, it has to do with depth, emotional depth. These guys can be so obsessed with the material world (Taurus) and the physical world (Sag) that they may forget to deal with matters of the heart and spirit. Just as both these men are prone to getting fat, eventually, because of their excessive appetites, they could also bring out a lazy, self-indulgent side of the other. They need to try hard to encourage each other's passions and desires to do something meaningful in life, instead of just focusing on lifestyle.

The Sag should encourage the Taurus man to explore his artistic abilities, especially the musical ones, and the Taurus should push his Sag lover to develop more of a real philosophy about life. In other words, Taurus, encourage your man to practice what he preaches. Don't just let him pontificate over a pitcher at the bar.

It's called work, sweeties, and you are both capable of it, so don't let the other get off easy, and that holds true in bed as well as in life.

The enemy of this relationship is smugness, but the ally for this pairing is integrity. Both of these guys possess strong beliefs and values, and that's what they need to hold on to when periods of emptiness and ennui set in. I'm talking long term now, and if the other planets are in sync, these chaps can be lifetime lovers. In fact, the Taurus loves to dress the Sag in chaps on every possible occasion.

So think about this relationship and explore it on a deep level, boys. You can start like this: stop talking in clichés.

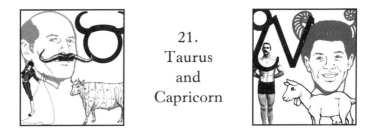

21.
Taurus
and
Capricorn

These two earth signs are divinely compatible and have a great potential to be together for years and years. Right from the start, there will probably be an attraction. The Taurus man likes that the Capricorn man is serious about his work and serious about sex. Mr. Taurus will take it upon himself to loosen up the Goat, who he believes is just a little too uptight and should enjoy himself more. Mr. Capricorn is, in turn, intrigued by the Bull's hedonistic inclinations, but he doesn't completely buy them. He knows that security and money are just as important to Mr. Taurus as they are to him.

Once involved, these two will find that they have similar rhythms. In life and in bed, they move at a similar, slow but steady earth-sign pace. The Capricorn man may be a little more driven and maniacal about attaining his goals, and the Taurus may be a bit more fun and lazy . . . preferring to watch movies and eat chips while the Capricorn is banging out reports and budgets on his laptop. But these differences just add to the relationship, since if they were too much alike, it would almost be incestuous.

The challenge for these earthy boys is in breaking out of the reliable routine they've developed together . . . at least once a decade. Once they get into a groove, they could find it hard to bust out of it. Neither likes change, and that can be the problem. Someone has to initiate movement in a new direction, once they've settled into a routine, or else they will wake up after a few years and "suddenly" find that their relationship is dead.

Rather than let that happen, each of them should make a concerted effort to delve into the unknown regularly. Meaning, Mr. Taurus should get out of his comfortable recliner and pick Mr. Capricorn's brain, the way an intense and curious Scorpio would. And Mr. Capricorn should be spontaneous and indulge some of the wild fantasies that Mr. Taurus has hinted at (probably having to do with food and dancing boys) and rock the Bull's world. If these two can summon up the energy and imagination, they can create a miracle of a love relationship that can really pass the test of time. And then the rest of us can just sit back and throw up, thrilled by how happy and satisfied they both are. I'm just kidding, actually. So long as they stay together, we will all have two favorite uncles to borrow money from and use as guarantors when looking for apartments. Alone, each is reliable and richer than we realize, but together they are solid . . . solid as a rock!

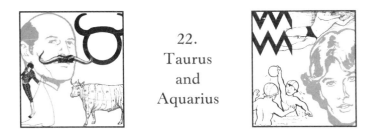

22.
Taurus
and
Aquarius

I am going to preface this section by saying that in my observation, the Taurus man begins with the upper hand in this pairing. The Taurus is so natural (and oblivious) that chances are he will just go about his business, being himself, while the hyperanalytical Aquarius uses his mind to obsess about the animal-like inclinations and behaviors of the primal Taurus. But the Taurus man is not the Java man, after all. Sooner than not, he'll pick up on the sexually obsessed vibe of the Aquarius. He'll ignore it, 'cause (unlike the Water Bearer) the Taurus doesn't like the unknown and is naturally resistant to it. But sooner or later his curiosity will get the better of him (even if it takes years) and he will want to experience what the most experiential sign in the zodiac is like . . . in bed.

This is a most unlikely duo, but therein lies the attraction. These men are as different as they come, but do share one important trait: stubbornness. That's why, if there's any hint of interest from either side, the man who wants to conquer (probably the Aquarius) will not give up until he has proven that he was right. Right about what? That sex between them is absolutely fantastic. And it is, my dears, it is. So why can't they just get along after they've gotten it on? Well, here we find another "square" situation. Their signs make a difficult square aspect to each other, and tend to grate on each other rather than bring out the best in both men.

Assuming there are enough aspects in their respective charts to give them a fighting chance, here's some insight into how to make this coupling really work. First of all, make sex the focus. That's right. None of this sweet-and-mushy malarkey or "process this and process that" baloney. Save that for your dykey sisters. You boys need to fuck like men and "talk things out" in one place: during the afterglow in each other's arms (okay, we can get a little sweet here). You see, there is something about this duo, I guess because they are from such different planets—Taurus being from gentle and artistic Venus and Aquarius being from change-loving and scientific Uranus—that neither man feels that he has much security in this relationship.

Mr. Taurus is always waiting for Mr. Aquarius to snap back into his strident intellectual mode and tell Mr. T, "It's over, and here's a typed dissertation explaining my rationale, in triplicate." And in the other corner, Mr. Aquarius is perpetually waiting for Mr. Taurus, an earthy "man's man," to announce, "I've figured out why you are so difficult to have a relationship with. You have no feelings. And I've found someone who has. Good-bye." And if they both fear being found out and left by the other, then you can bet that both men are aware of the first thing to go in any relationship: the sex. So if they can make the sexual arena their classroom and confession booth, they can make this bizarre but absolutely fascinating union last.

Oh, and remember that thing I mentioned about both being stubborn? Well, let me tell you, it will come in handy when both men pass the point of no return in love and want to make this relationship last forever. Neither one will be talking about leaving then (at least not seriously). They will work to make it work. No matter what it takes.

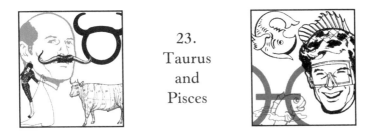

23.
Taurus
and
Pisces

This is a divine and easy kind of pairing, one that possesses it's own kind of unspoken magic. How does one put the unspoken into words? Well, that's what one diva lady astrologer will attempt to do! These two signs, you see, form a sextile to one another, a beneficial aspect. They have just enough in common to be naturally in sync and yet are different enough that each needs something from the other in order to feel whole. (To hell with that newfangled philosophy that says we all need to be whole ourselves rather than searching for someone else to complete us! These boys are from the old school of love . . . they're totally codependent, even if it's not fashionable anymore!)

These two may become lovers right away, or they may start out as friends. There is a natural kinship between the mutable water sign (Pisces) and the fixed earth sign (Taurus). If it's a friendship first, I'm sure that both will notice the romantic undertone in their "platonic" relationship. If one or both have a lover, the partners have every reason to be suspicious. There is just an undeniable chemistry here.

In bed, sparks will surely fly. Both men are incredibly sensual and dig having hours of foreplay before moving into more gritty X-rated territory. The Pisces man will encourage the Taurus to delve into a fantasy world with him, and the Bull is more than likely to dive in . . . because he trusts the Pisces so much.

What could cause a strain in the relationship, though, is that the Pisces tends to live his entire life in a fantasy world, populated by singing fairies (both gay and straight) who wear gossamer garb similar to that of Stevie Nicks and tell him how the world should be, not what it is. Meanwhile, the Taurus, once he has showered and gotten dressed, is Mr. Practical and absolutely *loves* to live in the material, concrete world. The Pisces (who is a not-so-closeted masochist, but is emotionally a very closeted sadist) may unconsciously provoke the Taurus into tormenting him. And the Taurus may withhold his sexual gusto if he gets tired of the Pisces man's convenient trips out of the land of reality, in their day-to-day lives.

The way for this relationship to last and last in a most beautiful manner is for each of these men to develop a latent trait that they both share: gentleness. With a little gentleness, Mr. Pisces can comfort Mr. Taurus during his times of worry by offering some concrete help and understanding. And Mr. Taurus, if he is gentle, can teach Mr. Pisces that the world outside their bedroom is not quite so scary and maybe even encourage the Fish to get more centered in reality.

Together, they can create a world where fantasy and reality overlap. And let me tell you, that is bound to be one sexy world.

24.
Gemini
and
Gemini

Two Gemini boys together spell one thing: mischief. Each Gemini will probably feel compelled to "one up" the other. When Gemini meets Gemini, you can bet that witty repartee and a subtle form of flirtation will fly. Who will make the first move, though? Probably the Gemini with the, shall we say, butcher planets (a moon in Aries there, a Leo or Taurus rising here). Chances are these boys will hit it off right away, although they could also annoy each other by *overdoing* the clever comments and coy repartee. I mean, enough is enough already!

Once safely in each other's arms, that's when the real test of compatibility begins. First of all, you can bet that, during their virgin encounter they will have to *do it* in an unusual place. A rooftop, the backseat of a car, or any dark street will do. Both will tend to overcompensate for their intellectual natures and express a wild sexual side. This could be more of a performance than the real thing, but by gum, it will still be a great experience.

At this point, if there is enough intrigue, and the relationship continues, it could go in any number of directions. Here are a few scenarios.

They could get serious quickly. And when I say "get serious," I mean they might start going out, chiefly to be seen, to all the hot spots. Each man by himself is a tremendous partyer (even if he's clean and sober and a born-again Christian, he still knows how to boogie!) and lover of the social scene.

Or they could get really serious, in the most serious of senses. These kids could hit it off so well, they move in together within a few months.

Or they could find that having their own most annoying qualities reflected back at them is too distressing, and they may end up calling it quits before it's even begun.

If they do start a real relationship, there will, of course, be a bright side and a dark side. The bright side is this: both boys are ruled by Mercury, the planet of communication, so they experience a true meeting of the minds and should be able to talk through their problems or disagreements. The darker side is tricky. You see, both men are so charming and easy to be with that they may not have any real "issues" with each other, but there may also not be any substance.

That is the true challenge for any pairing of Gemini and Gemini, finding the substance beneath the style.

25.
Gemini
and
Cancer

If anyone can warm up a cool Gemini gay man, it is the Cancer queen . . . I mean man. While Mr. Gemini is clever, funny, and social, Mr. Cancer is deep, warm, and tender. These boys are likely to admire each other and covet the endearing characteristics of the other. Mr. Cancer is loved by most because of his gentle and nurturing ways, but on some level he knows that he is laughed at behind his back for being a sap. Mr. Gemini is well aware of how impressive he is with a monologue at a party, but also knows deep down that if he were never born, no one would ever miss him. So when these two characters meet, they will probably sense, right off the bat, that they could be good for each other.

And they really could be. Just think what the Cancer man can do for the Gemini. He could bring out more feeling in this cool cat than forty husbands and eighty-six hustlers (all born under signs *other* than Cancer) could. In turn, the Gemini man could help the Cancer to temper his embarrassing sentimentality with true intelligence and wit.

So how's the sex, you ask? All right, dammit, here's the scoop: When these queer boys get together, there is likely to be some sweet heat right from the start. Chances are they will meet in a bar of some sort—the Cancer man being a big drunk (and even if he's in a recovery program, he's still a water sign and will want to drink seven seltzers before even saying hello) and the Gemini man being a major social butterfly. Before they go somewhere private, they will probably make out for a long, long time, since both love to kiss and neither is the "wham, bam, thank you, *man*" type. Sex itself will be quite passionate and surprisingly emotional. The Cancer is challenged by the Gemini man's anti-emotional vibe and will feel inspired to bring out his abilities to feel true lust *and* love, by making love to him in a most intense way. And Mr. Gemini loves to go along for the ride, so he will rise to the occasion and show some real feeling. When in Rome . . . or in this case, when with an emotional water sign . . . This is no act on his part either. Mr. Gemini could really get addicted to the deep, soulful loving he experiences with Mr. Cancer.

The main thing these fellows need to work on can be summed up in two words: *mood swings.* Cancer, of course, is ruled by the moon, which changes signs every couple of days, quicker than any other planet, and which explains why you can often find Mr. Cancer curled up alone in bed, crying for his mother's love on Wednesday, and maniacally club-hopping and holding court in front of a crowd of friends on Friday. And Mr. Gemini, ruled by the nervous planet Mercury, is such a nervous wreck on the inside, *all the time,* that he needs to do thirty things at once every minute, just to keep his senses in balance. So when these two moody guys are not in sync (which will be often), the fur could really fly.

The love between these boys could be real and lasting, but the day-to-day hysteria is bound to be just as fierce.

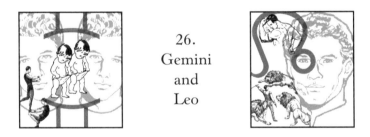

26.
Gemini
and
Leo

This pairing goes down as smooth and easy as a mint julep on a summer's day. Both of these boys are social, people-oriented, and basically happy types. The combination is sunny and optimistic. Although they each may have gone through periods of depression and dark despair (haven't we all, honey?) they both also possess a deep desire to enjoy life, rather than to revel in self-inflicted torment and angst (unless the Leo has a strong Scorpio influence or the Gemini a strong Pisces influence in their respective charts).

The Gemini man will recognize right away how much attention his Leo lover needs . . . and that is *a whole helluva lot,* sweeties! Mr.

Leo will adore being the big cheese in the relationship, the man in the spotlight. And Mr. Gemini will have no problem giving Mr. Leo what he wants. Mr. Gemini, after all, really doesn't like to be center stage. He much prefers sitting on the sidelines and making smart remarks and schmoozing with the paparazzi. Mr. Leo could in return give the ever wandering and flitty Gemini a sense of much needed consistency and security in his life. The Leo man will be protective and loving with his Gemini boyfriend. There is an unspoken loyalty between these guys, and everyone around them will see it.

Sexually speaking, this pair could either sizzle or sink. If there is real emotion between the two, sex could reach the heights of ecstasy. If the spark is forced, though, both will know it. Then it will just be a show. Remember, Gemini can wear many masks, and Leo is always the performer. Chances are, though, that something real and incredible could develop between these lads.

Mr. Gemini is likely to put Mr. Leo on a pedestal, which is exactly what both of them want! Mr. Gemini craves a romantic muse to gain inspiration from and a friend to bounce off of. Mr. Leo can be both and will love being treated like a queen . . . king . . . whatever!

Both boys should be aware of some potential pitfalls in their relationship as it develops. The Gemini tends to be cold and to go on emotional autopilot, which will not sit well with the Leo man, who demands that, if nothing else, his life mate must be *human!* The Leo, on the other hand, must curb his tendency to talk about himself and think about himself, *only,* twenty-four/seven. Mr. Gemini may make endearing jokes about Mr. Leo's ego, but real resentments will *really* build up if Mr. Leo doesn't check his ego at the door at least part of the time.

If both these fellows can remain friends on a basic level—and remember, no matter what else, they really *like* each other—then I have tremendous hopes for them. And if that's not enough, here's another incentive to stay together:

The Leo man is a major clotheshorse, and the Gemini man loves to wear costumes whenever the mood hits him. If their love lasts, just imagine the wardrobe they can accumulate if they put both their closets together!

27.
Gemini
and
Virgo

This pairing is full of paradoxes and surprises. Unpredictable is how I would describe any relationship between a Gemini man and a Virgo man. It's unusual right from the get-go because their signs make a square angle to each other, which is generally not such a fab thing. Squares are an aspect between two signs that are ninety degrees apart, and generally they are challenging and irritating and take a lot of work and patience by both people. *But,* both men are also ruled by quick-thinking Mercury, the planet of communication, which means they have more in common than any other "squared" pair in the zodiac. Mercury also assures that both fellows know how to articulate what is going on for them and that both can be objective enough to hear what the other person has to say.

Their sex life combines the elements of speed and subtlety. This is the area where they could really find the right groove. If the Virgo man gently thrusts his stomach (his erogenous zone) in the face of the Gemini man, you can bet that the Gemini will figure out eight different exciting things to do with that belly, using his hands, his mouth, and most of all his quick-thinking imagination, that will leave the Virgo man reeling. Similarly, the Virgo man is known for being a stickler for detail. So you can bet that if the Gemini man casually mentions over dinner an interest in motorcycles, the Virgo man will concoct a biker fantasy during that night's sexual escapades that will surprise and titillate his Gemini lover for hours on end.

The trouble could be that both these men are so mutable and adaptable that the relationship could go around in a circle without any clear direction. Of course if one or both have some cardinal signs in their chart (Aries, Cancer, Libra, or Capricorn), that will certainly help.

Both men also tend to be superanalytical, and not as comfortable dealing on an emotional plane. Gemini, of course, is a cerebral air sign, and Virgo is a practical earth sign. If one or both have some water or fire nicely placed in their charts, that will help a lot, too.

Overall, these two men are most likely to form a fantastic and lasting romantic relationship, if they develop their own type of language with each other. A language that only they can understand. For instance, if the Gemini man simply wants to read, he can say "Ciao" in just the right lighthearted, I-still-love-you-but-I-need-some-time-alone tone, and the Virgo man within a millisecond will busy himself by retiling the kitchen or grooming the dog, without making a big deal about it. And if the Virgo man needs for the Gemini man to be serious for a moment, he can say the special code word for that and his Gemini lover will stop playing and start listening.

And of course in bed, they can come up with lots of special codes for all the disgusting and wonderful things they will do together. Perhaps "paddle time" for a nice spanking and "get the butter" (as in *Last Tango in Paris*) for some nice raunchy butt-fucking. Oh, the possibilities are endless.

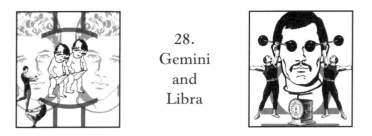

28.
Gemini
and
Libra

These two air signs have the potential to be deliriously happy together.

They both love to date and should have a grand old time painting the town red together, hanging out with mutual friends, going to parties (Gemini's influence) and artistic events (Libra's touch), and in general just being fabulous together.

Sexually, there is a definite spark between them. Both are flirty and elusive and will enjoy playing cat in mouse in the bedroom . . . and both will be the mice. Neither is easy to please, and therein lies the challenge. But this is a good challenge that both men will enjoy meeting. There is a curiously light feeling to sex, and neither one minds it that way. When their passions are sated, both will enjoy opening the window and letting the fresh air from outside cool their jets and cool their naked bodies. In their own airy way, these boys generate a lot of warmth. They just don't like to get all sticky and gushy about it (well, I mean emotionally!).

And as time passes, this could turn into something real and lasting. They are basically compatible and enjoy similar things in life and have similar daily rhythms. Each needs to be around people a lot, but also needs plenty of private time and space to clear his head and let his mind roam free . . . alone. The Libra is more romantic and can spoil the Gemini by showing him the pleasures of old-style romance, complete with candlelight, a walk on a moonlit beach, and handwritten love letters that reveal his innermost dreams and desires. The Gemini, in return, will be the companion the Libra has always wanted. Libras hate to feel lonely, more than any other sign, and with a Gemini that will rarely happen. The Gemini man will bring joy to the Libra's life by chatting naked with him about every subject under the sun till the dawn breaks, at which time Mr. Gemini will give Mr. Libra the rim job to end all rim jobs . . . all before breakfast.

The main challenge for these men can be described with one word that says it all yet says nothing at all (and therein lies the problem for these boys): *intimacy*. Each man tends to hold something back and see what the other is going to do. It is hard for both the Gemini man and the Libra man to be "all there," especially when times are tough. During an argument, it's as if four people are in the room: the Gemini man, the Libra man, and an alter ego for each of them who sits above, feeling removed and objective, saying, "Hmmm, interesting."

Since words are the tools that can tear this relationship apart or hold it together, I recommend that both men use their formidable language and communication skills to express their feelings, not to attack the other, and to tell the truth, not a convenient spin on the facts. If they can be real with one another, they can make each other very, very happy.

29.
Gemini
and
Scorpio

There is a certain "cat and mouse" feeling to this combination. "But who is the cat and who is the mouse?" you ask. Well, dear boys, that is an impossible question to answer when these two get together. Mr. Gemini and Mr. Scorpio have certain striking things in common. They both possess a scathing wit and an ability to crack people up or cut them down to size with sarcasm. Sarcasm, as all you pop psychologists know, can be a way to cover up anger and shoot it out at the universe (or more likely, the people closest to us) instead of expressing it directly. So when these two characters meet, it is likely to be a battle of words and stream-of-consciousness rants. Luckily, they will find each other to be formidable challengers and early on will probably greatly enjoy the banter that develops oh so naturally between them.

Mr. Gemini will add a lighter touch to their relationship. He's more playful and takes life (and himself) less seriously, after all. Mr. Scorpio knows that sometimes sparring is just a fascinating form of foreplay. The more Mr. Gemini keeps up with him, the more ready for some raunchy loving he will be.

And once these two do get it on, that is just the beginning of the fun. Both enjoy erotic surprises, which is why sex will rarely take place in bed, or in the usual positions. Mr. Gemini is definitely the more creative and flexible. He was after all a contortionist in a previous incarnation. Mr. Scorpio loves a challenge, though, and is also full of physical stamina when he is mentally turned on.

Once they've been dating for a while, a surprising sweetness develops between these two boys. They don't mind driving each other crazy and pushing each other's limits, but they become fiercely protective of the other if someone from outside their twisted little cocoon begins to pose a threat. Mr. Scorpio is especially protective of his Gemini boyfriend. If some bitchy queen or nasty boss tries to hurt the Gemini, the Scorpio man will poise himself to attack within a heartbeat.

It's during a moment of crisis or a turning point that the real stuff this relationship is made of comes out. Since both are drawn to great mysteries that can only be explored sexually, the issue of monogamy is bound to come up early and be an important one.

This kind of relationship can only be monogamous, and therein lies the rub. Mr. Gemini, surprisingly, has no problem, when push comes to shove, agreeing to a one-on-one-only relationship, and he will stick to it. But will all his needs be met? He may feel safe with Mr. Scorpio, but he may also feel trapped and misunderstood. A lot depends on the other planetary aspects here. Mr. Scorpio may want more intensity than he can get from Mr. Gemini, and when he realizes that, he may start to act quite mean toward his light-spirited Gemini lover.

The best relationship between these two signs will occur under three possible circumstances:

(1) If their other planets are intensely compatible (a Scorpio moon for the Gemini, perhaps; a Libra rising for the Scorp; etc.).
(2) If they have known each other for a long time before getting involved.
(3) If both have lived through relationships that have taught them about what they do want from a lover and what they can't deal with.

30.
Gemini
and
Sagittarius

The chemistry between these men, born under opposite signs, is palpable. Both Gemini and Sag are mutable signs, which means they are naturally *adaptable*. They will get a sense of the other right away, and both will give a little bit to make the other feel more comfortable. Mr. Gemini is great at witty banter and will get the conversation rolling right away. Mr. Sagittarius will do his part by becoming immediately *physical* with his Gemini buddy. There is just something very friendly about this pair. So friendly that it is no surprise when a friendly tweak of a nipple turns to mad humping in the closet at a mutual friend's party during the first night of their meeting.

Sexually, these two fit together well. The Gemini knows he is the smarter one, or at least quicker with his tongue (in every sense), so he is likely to lead the Sag into the activities that turn the Gemini on most. Something about the Sag's obvious or latent manly ways will make the Gemini want to be dominated by the loose-cannon Sag. The Sagittarius man is fine with that, but his ultimate goal is to get the Gemini man to stop thinking so bloody much, to get out of his head and into his heart and body. No mean feat, but if anyone can do it, it's the man born under the sign of the Archer. If he has his sights set on a Gemini, he will stop at nothing to conquer him in all the best possible senses.

Once this relationship picks up steam, what happens then? Well, day to day, they are compatible enough. Both men like to have the freedom to do their own things. Mr. Gemini has lots of friends and intellectual interests that take up a lot of his time. And Mr. Sag has his interests, too: eating, gambling, partying. Yes, he does love excess!

But by night they will get together and meet on common ground. They are both social creatures. Chances are they will squeeze in some time for love either before, during, or after going out in public. Neither man wants to be a hermit, and each has primal fears of losing his freedom.

So the real challenge for these boys is, how do two freedom-loving types stay in a relationship together? The word *relationship* of course implies certain restrictions. Well, it's easier than you might think, though sometimes the simplest things in theory (my dear pontificating Sag friend) can be the hardest to put into practice (my too clever for your own good Gemini pal). They must constantly *talk*. The Sag is honest but dense, and the Gemini is smart but tricky, so they need to talk more than the average duo to understand each other. But these boys are not a couple of liberal straight people or process-oriented lesbians, after all, so they also need to *get it on* as often as they talk things through. A healthy combination of sex and self-psychology will make this a relationship that can last a lifetime.

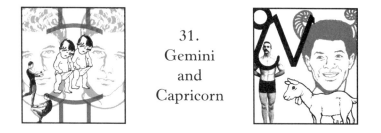

31.
Gemini
and
Capricorn

Ah, what a strange duo we have here. The Gemini man is likely to get the ball rolling and flirt madly (but coyly) with the Capricorn. Something about the Capricorn's silent nature will be oddly endearing and ever so challenging to the talkative and nervous Gemini boy. Now keep in mind, these two fellows come from different worlds. The Capricorn man is a practical, cardinal earth sign. He only believes what he sees and would even then prefer something notarized and sealed and locked away in his safety-deposit box as proof. So at first, he is unlikely to trust the mercurial and mutable air-sign flightiness of the Gemini man.

Of course, that won't prevent them from sleeping together. And a lot of things could happen once the lights are low and the pants come off. Mr. C could feel a little shy and inhibited around the Gemini man and might expect the Gemini to take the lead in bed. If that happens, you've got a recipe for disaster, because the Gemini man is so much better at bouncing off someone else rather than leading his lover into unknown territory. Or the Capricorn man could take his Gemini lover to some dark and intense places. The Capricorn man loves a little bondage and over-the-top violence in the bedroom. He's so bloody pent up by day and obsessed with his career that he simply *must* find an outlet for all those "inappropriate" feelings and desires. And what better outlet than Mr. Gemini's all too willing butt? This could be fun for the Capricorn, but after a while could become tedious for the Gemini, who hates repetition.

The Capricorn and the Gemini might also explore a variety of twisted but exciting sexual exploits with each other, and both maintain their sense of humor throughout. If the Capricorn man can learn to laugh at himself and his own "demons" (ooooh! scary!) and the Gemini man can laugh at himself for being such a ditsy queen, the two of them can actually let their inhibitions down and enjoy an incredibly powerful sex life.

That in itself is not going to be easy. These men are unlikely to trust each other or to give each other a break initially. They are just such different animals. But if and when they do establish trust— enough to expose themselves in an intimate, sexual way—then comes the issue of trust on an emotional level.

Can they both let down their guard enough to really bare their souls to one another? Hard to say. If one or both of them have a good bit of Taurus or Cancer, that would certainly help. But even if the desire is there, trust and the laying open of hearts will have to wait a little while . . . at least until they see if they even *like* each other.

If they have some things in common, that is a good sign. But what would boys like this have in common with each other? The word that comes to mind for both Gemini and Capricorn is *industrious*. Neither of these men like to just sit around without a plan. Mr. Gemini needs to use his quicksilver mind (and dexterous hands) all the time, while Mr. Capricorn always needs to have a purpose. If they can harness Mr. Gemini's mental energy and Mr. Capricorn's drive and direct them toward common goals and interests, they can be two happy playmates together.

32.
Gemini
and
Aquarius

This pair is generally quite compatible. Both men place a high value on friendship, and that deep "brotherly" connection will hold them together even if there is no strong physical attraction right off the bat. And while we're on the subject . . . what is the glue (or other sticky substance) that holds these mates to each other sexually? Well, both men are naturally cool . . . and oddly, never seem to sweat. That's why their friends can't help but laugh when the boys talk about how "hot" their sex life is. No one else can see it. And most of their pals are likely to laugh at their "animal passion" for each other. Please, Mary!

But it is there.

The Aquarius man is attracted to the Gemini's bimbo-esque ways, but suspects something deeper and darker is going on underneath Mr. G's calm, *cool* facade. And while the Gemini man may laugh at how seriously his Aquarius lover takes himself and the world, he does respect the man's integrity. But he also wants to test it.

Example:

AQUARIUS (*high and mighty*): I am a complete vegetarian. I don't think we have any right to cruelly slaughter animals and eat them for our pleasure.

GEMINI (*flip*): Those are nice leather boots you're wearing.

AQUARIUS (*flustered and humorless*): Hey! I'm not perfect. At least I'm *trying* to cut down on the amount of torture animals are put through. And besides, these boots were a present!

GEMINI: Why don't you give me a little present and I won't tell anybody what a hypocrite you are.

And from this comes a little boots-and-saddle scene reminiscent of the Castro in its seventies heyday.

You get the picture. These boys don't let each other get away with anything. That's all part of the fun for them. But after the semikinky sex and the bright dialogue is done, what then? What happens as months pass and the relationship becomes serious? Well, it's either one way or another for these boys. If all they can do is repeat the above-mentioned scene with different dialogue and different fetishes, this union will not last. It will turn into a friendship, which is not a bad thing, for in general these guys can be a real force of good for each other. But for them to cross over into a real soul-mate realm, there has got to be *a lot* more emotion. Since both air-sign men tend to live in their heads most of the time, one (or both) of them had better have some water or fire in his chart to bring out some real passion and feeling. If they can start arguing about things they really care about and not have just "fill in the blank" type discussions, then they are going to be hooked on each other for life.

Example:

AQUARIUS: I am sick of the way women in our society are exploited.

GEMINI: Don't you pay your female employee less than you pay your male employee?

AQUARIUS: She has less experience.

GEMINI: Just like your mother.

AQUARIUS: What's that supposed to mean?

GEMINI: Didn't your mother get the short end of the stick at her company for years and years while you were growing up?

AQUARIUS: I'm giving Angela a raise.

GEMINI: What? You don't have to prove anything to me. I was just giving you a hard time.

AQUARIUS: Well, I'm glad you did. I refuse to put another woman through what my mother went through.

GEMINI: But if you give her a raise, how are you going to afford to take me to Hawaii over Christmas?

AQUARIUS: I don't want to make you feel like a whore. We'll both pay our own way.

GEMINI: But I want to feel like a whore!

It's a subtle difference, but it's there, dear astrological students of the human psyche. You see, if both these men can cut past the pontificating (Aquarius) and glib sarcasm (Gemini), they can each torture . . . I mean *help* the other on a more personal level. But unlike if either of them were having this argument with a Scorpio (who fights dirty) or a Cancer (who overloads the guilt), the playing field is fair. And at the end of it all, a nice little prostitute role-play or locker-room scene will end the discussion on a pleasurable note.

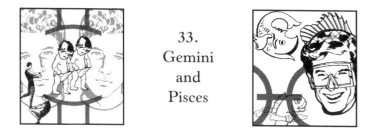

33.
Gemini
and
Pisces

There is something dreamy about this duo. They could have a lot of fun together and discover a deep emotional connection, to boot . . . or they could simply drive each other crazy. Let's take a closer look, shall we? (Don't answer that, Gemini . . . I know you have a short attention span!) Both Gemini and Pisces are mutable signs, and *mutable* in astrological terms means wimpy . . . uh, I mean flexible, and adaptable. Both these boys have probably already had romantic relationships of one sort or another with fixed signs (Taurus, Leo, Scorpio, or Aquarius), who are reliable but dominating, and cardinal signs (Aries, Cancer, Libra, or Capricorn), who are good at initiating matters but not so good at knowing what to do once they've started the ball rolling.

This combination of the two most mutable of mutable signs (Sagittarius is the impulsive mutable sign and possesses a lot of get-up-and-go fire energy, and Virgo is the hardworking mutable sign who can't bear letting his earth-sign industriousness go to waste) is something of a divine experiment.

Chances are the more romantic Pisces will take the first aggressive step toward the Gemini. Pisces, ruled by Neptune, is full of illusions about himself and about every cute guy he meets. The Pisces man will probably do a bit of magical thinking when he first meets the Gemini man. What the rest of us might read as "shallow" in the Gemini man, the Pisces will read as "deep."

Example:

GEMINI: Did you read that new book about Princess Diana? I couldn't believe they put such an unattractive picture of her on the cover . . . wearing sweats, with her hair all a mess. I was horrified.

PISCES *(thinks to himself)*: *Wow, he can't bear the thought of a dead legend being humiliated.*

In reality the Gemini man would have been horrified to see anybody attired in gym clothes out in public.

Of course, the Gemini man may have his own illusions about the Pisces man. The "mystery" of Mr. Pisces, which the rest of us see as his confusion, Mr. Gemini may see as "intelligence."

Example:

GEMINI: What do you think that Picasso painting means?

PISCES *(after a long, long pause)*: Look at that woman. *(Ominously) Look* at that woman.

GEMINI: Yeah. *(Thinks to himself) Why can't I see what is going on deep in her soul? He is so smart!*

In reality, you and I know that the Pisces man doesn't have a clue what is going on, he's just lost in his thoughts and, after a full minute's passed, can't even remember the Gemini's question.

Sexually, this combination definitely has the potential to be dreamy and steamy. These boys bring out the experimental side in each other, and both are incredibly imaginative. Sex will become more challenging when the novelty wears off. In layman's terms, when the effects of the enemas and the circus paraphernalia are over with, what can they do to top their wildest fantasies?

Emotionally, the question is, when they get past their illusions about each other, will they really like or even love what they see?

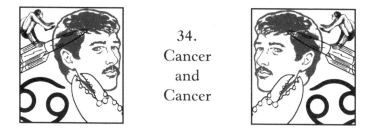

34.
Cancer
and
Cancer

This is a cuddly, cute, and clingy little combination, if ever I saw one! Both men are the marrying kind. The sign Cancer, of course, rules *family*, specifically the role of mother. I don't care how butch on the outside any Cancer man is, on the inside he is just a big baby, who often nurtures and protects like a big mama.

The emotional connection between these men is the most important factor in their relationship, right from the start. And if they can get past their natural defensiveness and distrust of strangers, they are likely to hit it off in a meaningful way pretty quickly. They do, after all, share the same values and many of the same interests. Both are likely to love good food, the water, sports, watching TV, eating, going to the beach, going out to eat, playing outside, etc. Oh, and they both love repetition.

In bed, they will probably devour each other. Sex is like a delicious meal to both Cancer men. And even when it's not delicious, they still hope it will be. Drinking is often a favorite pastime of the Cancer man, so there is likely to be a lot of drunken, debaucherous sex during the early part of their relationship.

The truth will come out when they hit a rough patch. When a Cancer man is going through a difficult time, it will be even more difficult for him to talk about it. He is deeply shy and easily embarrassed and is much more likely to withdraw or act out rather than talk about his problems. If the other Cancer man is smart, he will sense this and draw his Cancer boyfriend out of his shell and treat him with kid gloves. If either Cancer man is too emotionally rough on the other, forget it. The clock will be ticking on their relationship from that point on.

Hopefully, since both men are so naturally sensitive and loving, each can put his mood swings aside and take care of the other.

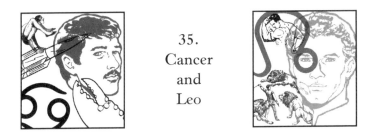

35.
Cancer
and
Leo

This combination has a lot of potential. Certainly, the one thing that comes to mind when I think of both these men is affection. Practically all men, even my dear darling gay boys, are taught in subtle or often not so subtle ways to hold back their emotions and not express them. Luckily, both the Cancer man and the Leo man just can't help but reach out and literally touch the people they care about and express their innate warmth and capacity to love, in obvious, wonderful physical ways.

So chances are, if there is a physical and emotional attraction between these two, they won't waste time playing games. They will do a lot of hugging and hand-holding and shoulder grabbing, right in front of everybody . . . which will then quite easily lead to lots of nipple pinching, thigh licking, and butt humping behind closed doors. (I know you Leo boys like to show off in front of an audience, but the Cancer man isn't the media whore you are . . . at least not when it comes to his sex life.)

Both men are creative and warm, which (if you add in the fact that they're *gay*) is likely to make them both artists of some sort. Chances are, a mutual interest in the arts will bring them together. They are both practical and security-minded, too, so both may work in the business of art, rather than on the pure creative side, but you never know. These boys may bring out the true artiste in each other.

They are both romantic and will probably show their affection through cards and special gifts. Food is love to each of them, although chances are, practical Mama Cancer will want to cook at home, while big-spending Leo will prefer to eat out. Either way, food will be a big aphrodisiac for both.

The trouble between these gents could be this: neither of them possesses any objectivity whatsoever. Cancer is so moody and self-conscious (all right, paranoid!) that he thinks the mailman is laughing at him and belittling him when he gets the same coupon batch that everybody else gets in the mail. Can you imagine how paranoid he can be when his mate makes an insensitive remark? And the Leo man is so proud and so self-absorbed he may barely have time to listen to his Cancer boyfriend, because he is so concerned with whether *he* is being heard. What is wrong with them?

Damned if I know, but if these two can create their own little self-involved world of sensual miracles and petty slights, and accept the contradictions within it, they could be happy together.

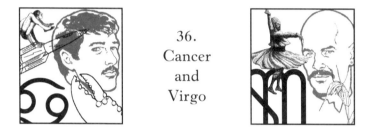

36.
Cancer
and
Virgo

This can be a winning, easy, and natural combination, provided that each man learns the other's rules early on. Both men are neurotic. That's a given. And most of their neuroses are played out in the home. That's why I suggest they check out each other's pads right at the beginning of the relationship. Mr. Cancer probably lives with his mother or has some bizarre, temporary setup. Perhaps he lives in the back of a bodega with six cats and three pregnant (human) roommates all of whom he is Lamaze partner for. Why so strange? It's not a lack of money, probably. This man knows how to work and how to save. It's all because he can only make a real home with a real husband . . . which is what he's looking for. Will he find it in Mr. Virgo? Well, let's take a look at the "Virgin" Mary. The Virgo man is full of phobias and fantasies, and if you look around his crib, you can figure them out (he's pretty transparent). Let's see, a nurse's uniform in the closet, a leather hood in the sock drawer, and in every room an air purifier turned up so high you can barely hear yourself think. Sounds about right. I may be making light of their shtick, but believe me, they take themselves very seriously.

Sexually, the main job each has is to loosen the other's inhibitions. Luckily, both have such strange but adorable mental problems that sex is bound to be quite hot and bizarre. They are both so tied up in knots emotionally, they are likely to revel in ecstasy once they get the chance to blow, er . . . off steam with one another.

Down the road, they can make quite a happy little home together. Both are serious and will either jump from dating to "it's destiny" and move in together faster than you can say "two lesbians and a U-Haul" or be frightened away by the idea of committing to someone as nutty as they are. If they choose to hitch up, the odds are good that this relationship could last and thrive.

Although they have a lot of similarities, it's the ways that they are different that will serve this relationship best. Mr. Virgo is ruled by communicative Mercury and will be able to articulate his feelings and to help Mr. Cancer to do the same. The Cancer man will be able to soothe and comfort his Virgo lover's frayed nerves. And the Virgo man will be moved when he sees that, finally, he has found someone to take care of him. They will protect each other from all outside forces, and both men should be quite loyal (unless of course the Virgo is young or has a Sagittarius moon, or the Cancer has too much Libra in his chart). Their home is probably a great place to visit, but I sure wouldn't want to live there. No offense, boys. I wish you well in your own little bizarro universe. (And I know yours is the first place I would go to if I was in desperate need of an aloe face mask or a thimbleful of nutmeg.)

37.
Cancer
and
Libra

These men, both born under cardinal (leadership-oriented) signs, are both gentle and deeply sensitive. Yes, the Cancer man may show a lot of chutzpah and self-will, but this same little toughie can turn to mush when he receives a sentimental Valentine's Day card. And though the air-ruled (i.e., supercerebral, anti-emotional) Libra man may have an intellectual rationalization for every question from "Is love real?" to "Are poor manners justification for execution?" he, too, will get all soppy when he is taken to a romantic place and wooed like a woman!

Together, these boys are just a pair of old softies, but whether or not they are truly compatible depends a lot on their whole charts. Again, with this pair we find two men whose Sun signs are at a harsh, square angle to each other. Yes, they can certainly learn a lot from each other. No question about that. But will they enjoy spending almost every day and night together? That is a question that they will find an answer to pretty early on in their relationship, because both enjoy playing house and will want to do so right away.

Playing house of course involves sharing a bed.

Sexually, these two remind me of a song from *A Chorus Line*, "Tits and Ass," because Cancer rules the former and Libra rules the latter. There is a certain beautiful simplicity and genuine romance and sincerity to their lovemaking. And it is *love*making, even if the relationship lasts a fraction of the time that the aforementioned show lasted on Broadway. Neither is a size queen when it comes to the length of a relationship. With each other, both Mr. Cancer and Mr. Libra fantasize, "Could this be the one?"

This relationship could be the one for both of them if they are at a stage in life where both are really grown-up enough to settle down. Libra, after all, is the sign of marriage, and Cancer is the sign of family. If both men have done enough living and self-reflection to know themselves, then they will be ready to open their heart to each other.

Of course if both boys are young and still forming emotionally, they could still have quite a beautiful affair. I picture them getting together while each is alone on vacation (but perhaps I am too romantic . . . chances are, both have a lover waiting for them on the other side of the island). They meet, they make love on the beach, they share their hopes and dreams with each other, exchange rings and vows, then go back home to their real lives. Even if it doesn't last forever, they will always have incredible dreamlike memories of each other, and their special week in Cancún. (Yes, each of these boys is a closet conservative and is likely to enjoy slumming with straight folks.)

Love, however, could last forever between Mr. Cancer and Mr. Libra if they can somehow combine the dreamlike quality of their romance with the serious commitment that both men crave.

38.
Cancer
and
Scorpio

These two water signs are generally compatible in a most immediate and intense way, and many can create lasting relationships with one another. Since watery people tend to be moody and introverted, neither should take for granted that he "knows" the other in an in-depth way . . . even after years together! With that disclaimer off my chest, read on, my dear homosexuals.

Right off the bat, there is bound to be a current of electricity that runs between these fellows. The Scorpio man is apt to *seem* like the aggressor, but I bet you a seafood dinner that he is just playing off the Cancer man's coy, obvious, and completely charming cues. The Scorpio man will probably have a huge appetite for his Cancer lover. He will love chasing after the coquettish Cancer boy, who will in turn love being ravaged.

Their sex life is bound to be fantastic but also unpredictable and sometimes loaded in a most frightening way. You see, both men are moody and not always so talented at connecting where their "black" moods are coming from. Lashing out at each other, especially in response to a perceived "lack of sensitivity" in bed, may happen on occasion.

Example:

SCORPIO: Why did you stop?

CANCER: That is so typical of you! You don't even care about how *I* feel!

SCORPIO: How *do* you feel?

CANCER: Oh, don't try to make this all about me!

SCORPIO: What about me? I'm getting a little sick of your
emotional histrionics right when I'm about to come!
CANCER: You are such an animal!
SCORPIO: I'll show what an animal I am . . .

Yes, they are lovably ridiculous. The Cancer is supermoody, and
the Scorpio has more of a "fire sign" temper than the other water
signs. One way or another, the water will boil with these two. And
although sex can be a roller coaster of emotion (as we saw in the
preceding dramatization), the problems these two may face will have
little or nothing to do with their bedroom antics.

No, the challenge in a relationship between Mr. Cancer and Mr.
Scorpio is this: both tend to withdraw into a deep, deep emotional
place where each can hide from himself as well as his lover. During
the early, getting-to-know-you honeymoon phase of the relationship,
this is not an issue. They are apt to love, talk, fight, dream, and
fuck like bunnies (well, at least I think bunnies do all of the above).
But as they grow more set in their ways, and set in their couple-y
routines, they could grow apart. So long as both men are growing
together and moving toward similar destinations in life, I am sure
they can be very happy and weather life's storms with love and
humor. But if Mr. Cancer really wants to raise a family and write
his great American novel in the cornfields of Iowa, and Mr. Scorpio
wants to conquer Wall Street and enjoy café society in New York,
they've got a problem. The key is for both to drag the "ugly" truth
out of each other very, very regularly (like every day). If their
dreams stay in sync, they could experience a love to end all loves.

39.
Cancer
and
Sagittarius

These men have the best chance at happiness together if they have
one of the following obsessions in common: sports or food. Some-

thing about this pair conjures up for me an image of two straight men having a relationship. The Sag man is undoubtedly boisterous and fond of the great outdoors (unless he's the egghead sort with every other planet in an air sign), and the Cancer man, too, will probably have a soft spot for Mother Nature. Rather than obsess about their careers as do most folks today—particularly those of us who were born while Pluto was in workaholic Virgo (from August 20, 1957, to July 30, 1972)—these fellows know that life is for living. So even if they are Pluto in Virgo types, they can still take a weekend off and enjoy stuffing themselves with food, hiking up a mountain, boinking to their heart's content, then doing it all again the next day.

Sexually, this pair has some great things going for them, but some drawbacks they should be aware of, too. Let's start with the challenges these giddy boys may face, and let me describe it the way I would plug their sitcom:

"What happens when a hypersensitive mama's boy meets a bigmouthed, tactless lout and they decide to become each other's boy toy? The answers are sure to be zany on *Saggey and the (Cancer) Man*, Thursdays at nine!"

So, Mr. Sag, if you can remember that pointing to something unusual on your Cancer lover's body and laughingly screaming "What's that!" is considered tactless, you will score many points in round one in the romance arena.

But, Mr. Cancer, you, too, can do me and yourself a favor by developing what we, in the developed world, call . . . I'll say it slowly . . . "a sense of humor." Your Sag lover may innocently make you cringe by speaking before thinking, but he is just as capable of laughing at himself as he is of laughing at you, so please, lighten up!

Okay, bad stuff out of the way, here's the good news.

In bed, these boys are like two pups, cubs, or any young animals that enjoy serious humping. Sex is divinely *physical* between them, and nourishing, too. Sexually, they meet on an even playing field, and each brings out a side in the other that is rare and rarely seen.

Mr. Sag can make the normally quiet and self-conscious Cancer scream like the hapless slut-victim in an early-eighties slasher film. Mr. Cancer can make the normally all-action-no-feeling Sag man actually swoon in sensual ecstasy (you guessed it) *like a woman.*

As for a long-term relationship, there are definite possibilities. Both of these guys are fun loving and enjoy the simple things in life (which is what makes their excesses so exhilarating!), but I have a feeling they would be best suited for marriage if both men have been around the block many a time before they exchange vows. If not, they could both act like a straight man and trade each other in for a younger model after several years of togetherness.

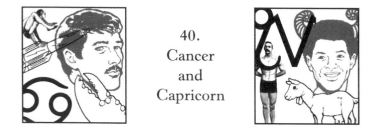

40.
Cancer
and
Capricorn

Ah, here we return to the land of opposites, this time of the cardinal persuasion, cardinal in astrology representing initiative, leadership abilities, and pushiness. How are they pushy? is the question, of course. Mr. Cancer is pushy about traditionally girly things such as his feelings. The crabby man insists that the people around him be sensitive to his moods and feelings at all times. Mr. Capricorn, born under the sign that represents the father, is pushy about what daddies are most obsessed with (besides prostitutes): *career.* As you can already see, there is a certain yin-yang balance to their relationship.

Chances are, with these boys, opposites will attract. Although most people (include Mr. Cancer's highly protective pals) will view Mr. Capricorn as a bit of cold fish, and perhaps even an opportunist, Mr. Cancer will see something much deeper and more endearing in this hard-to-read man. He will dig the Capricorn man's dignity (even when Sir Cappy is down on all fours begging to be whipped harder) and his work ethic (who else would plow away at Mr. Cancer for hours, patiently allowing him to come at his own pace?). Mr.

Capricorn will be drawn to Mr. Cancer's nurturing and affectionate nature. Capricorns can be affectionate, too, if they are taught how, you know!

In bed they share a perverse fascination with early childhood that comes out in ways that children should not be allowed to read about! The Capricorn's natural sadism meshes ever so well with the Cancer's innate masochism.

Of course both may be too uptight or (gasp!) just plain uninterested in anything too kinky, in which case they may get into traditional hetero roles in bed . . . which in itself I think is the kinkiest variation of all! Whoever is the top (Cancer, more likely) will want to fuck hard regularly, then roll over and go to sleep. The bottom (probably the Capricorn) will enjoy the challenge of forcing her . . . I mean *his* lover to prolong the ecstasy. Throw in a joint checking account, a couple of kids, and a corporate job for the designated hubby, and you've got *Father Knows Best* all over again.

On an emotional level, the issue that will bring them together or tear them apart (or both, depending on transits, progressions, natal charts, and the unmeasurable mystery of human nature) is *trust*. I'm not talking about trust in relation to fidelity. Those "who's zoomin' who" issues can be worked out over time. I'm talking about the deep, dark secrets, stemming back to when they were both wee and innocent children, that each man is afraid to reveal to himself let alone to another person.

Can the Capricorn man prove to the Cancer man over time that he will reserve judgment and be open and loving and supportive if and when the Cancer man feels safe enough to show his wounds? In fact, can Capricorn coax his Cancer lover out of his shell, rather than waiting and waiting until it's too late? Can the Cancer man evolve enough to put love first and his reactions second? In fact, can he put his own "let me make this about me" reactions aside altogether? If these men can answer yes to all of the above, then they are made for each other and can celebrate that they have found their other halves.

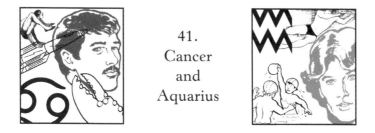

41.
Cancer
and
Aquarius

What could these two men possibly have in common? On first glance, not a lot. Their styles are so vastly different. On the surface, Mr. Aquarius is an analytical, highly opinionated, principled man who believes what he sees, rather than what he feels. Mr. Cancer is a mess of emotions who somehow manages to inspire the cuddly warmth of all of those around him. It's Mr. Wizard meets Mr. Rogers. Or in gay terms, Mr. Wizard blows Mr. Rogers.

Either way, it is not who they are as individuals that defines this relationship; it is the unique entity they create when they become lovers. Mr. Cancer can soften Mr. Aquarius's harsh edges, with a lot of hugs and home-cooked meals. Mr. Aquarius can hush the hysterics of high-strung Mr. Cancer by calmly talking to him, listening and bringing an objective point of view.

In bed, however, all labels get dropped. The traditional Cancer man will have his mind (and other parts of his anatomy) expanded by the kinky and creative Aquarius man. And in turn the Cancer man will gently persuade his Aquarius man to drop all his gimmicks and just feel pure, unadulterated pleasure *and* emotion. Just add water sports and you've got lifelong sexual compatibility.

Day to day, they could find each other's differences quite appealing. The Aquarius man adores his friends and makes them a top priority, while the Cancer man tends to isolate himself from all the platonic pals who adore him. Mr. Aquarius can teach Mr. Cancer how to be a good friend, and this is a gift that the deeply loving, but sometimes uncommunicative Crab man will find priceless. In turn, Mr. Cancer, who knows that family is forever, will teach the distancing and cold Aquarius, who does his duty by his family, but no more, how to feel real compassion for his kin . . . even his nut job of a mother. And for this, although he may never admit it, Mr.

Aquarius will be forever indebted to his Cancer lover. After all, if the Aquarian can find good in his crazy family, he can find good in anybody. This is major because the Aquarius man likes to practice what he preaches, and he preaches loving all man (and woman) kind.

However, I do paint a rosy picture, dear boys. This couple will face definite challenges. When arguing, the Cancer will undoubtedly resort to personal attacks of a childish nature: "I don't like the way you smell!" and the Aquarius man will shut off and go into judgment mode, which could make everyone within a three-hundred-mile radius feel as if a cold front has just stormed into town.

They need to put their own less than perfect languages aside and create a new one that works just for them. If Ronald (Aquarius) Reagan and his wife Nancy the Cancer could do it, so can these boys. And the dear lady in red was an astrology buff, too!

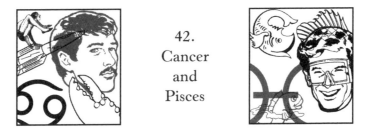

42.
Cancer
and
Pisces

These two water-sign men have the potential to make a magical couple together. In fact, both may send out the wedding invitations and buy a co-op together before they even find out each other's middle name. Let me fill the boys in on those details right now. It's Mr. Cancer "Clingy" Man and Mr. Pisces "Manipulative" Man. All right, those are their middle names on bad days. On good days it's Mr. Cancer "Heroic" Man and Mr. Pisces "Saintly" Man. (That's Saint-*ly* not Saint *party*, by the way.) The problem right from the start is that these guys can dig each other so much that they may both just *assume* that they know everything about the other within the first two weeks. And we all know what happens when we assume.

This little problem is understandable, though, when you see how much good they have between them as a couple. Sexually, they can do the dirtiest things together, all in the name of love. And a shower or bath before, during, or after their lovin' makes them both pure again.

No one else can give tender loving attention to Mr. Pisces's much talked about and incredibly sensitive feet the way Mr. Cancer can, while simultaneously giving him the bang of a lifetime. And no one can worship the sexy and erotically charged chest of a Cancer man the way a Pisces man can, and in so many ways! Oh, their pillow talk, presex dirty talk, and breakfast-the-day-after smug talk is sweet all right.

It's the reality part of their relationship that could be the challenge. When all the cutesy, sweetie-honey, fuck-me-Daddy, lovey-dovey stuff has dried up (say at about 3 P.M. on a Monday), they may find themselves feeling oddly unconnected to each other.

What to do? Well, the Pisces man should take a lesson from his Cancer boyfriend, who is more capable of being practical and of managing in the real world. The Cancer man, though, should try to emulate his Pisces lover's open, flexible nature.

And both should realize that they are dealing with a water-sign lover. Love and sex will be deep, passionate, and meaningful, but fraught with big scary waves, and depressing low tides. If both men have the courage to ride through the different waters, and to look deep into the stormy eyes of the other man, then they could experience a love that is truly magical, *and* truly real.

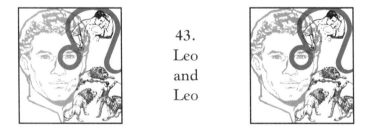

43.
Leo
and
Leo

These boys are in love with love, and the big, bawdy, beautiful glamour of romance with a capital *R*. Leo men are lovably naive, and lovably loving, so even when they've been burned in romance, they can still open their hearts again and again. The question is, can two Leos fall in love with each other? The obvious answer is yes, and the obvious answer is all most "big picture" Leo men need. If one Leo man is attracted to another, all he really needs to do is use flattery, old-fashioned romancin' tactics (flowers, candy, bondage), and his own iron will. For what a Leo wants, a Leo always gets.

All right, so let's say these boys have made it to round one: mutual nudity. What then? Well, I am not here to act as an instruction manual for gay male sex (unless the price is right, sweeties). But let's just say once they are in bed, the sparks should crackle, then fly. These two men really know how to make slow love. They are both lovers of luxury, so if they can have their first few encounters in a four-star hotel with a heart-shaped Jacuzzi (tacky is fine!), then they will be off to a magnificent start.

Can they get along over time? It's either a big yes or a big no. If one of them is less in love than the other, it's just a matter of time until he writes a big "Dear Leo" letter to the other poor sap. But if there are enough compelling differences in their charts to bring them together and inspire them to stick together, here are some tips for daily living.

Don't bark orders! Leos run a tight ship, but most people don't like living with a Navy SEAL (unless she looks like Demi Moore, pre–plastic surgery, during her *St. Elmo's Fire* film-acting peak . . . but that's in my book for girls). So, boys, please try to ask nicely and speak in a growly, sexy voice not a shrill, retired-Florida-matron tone.

Try new things in bed! Leo is a traditional kind of sign. Usually, a Leo man will get "brought out" into a deeper, more imaginative side of his sexuality by another man who is less inhibited and more adventurous. Two Leo men together run the risk of making a stodgy pair of lovers. Promise each other you'll visit the sex-toy shop every month on your monthly anniversary (Leos love to celebrate), and subscribe to at least one or two porn magazines.

A lot depends on the other planets in their charts, but the one thing these two do have in common is the fixed and unchangeable fact that they believe in love and they believe in loyalty. Seems like a pretty good start to me. Now take your clothes off, boys, and let nature take its course.

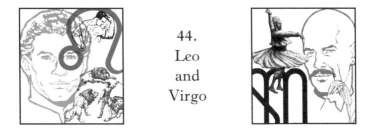

44.
Leo
and
Virgo

This is one of the combinations that I recommend this recipe to: go out on three dates, and if you (either of you!) still want to look at the other in the morning, then keep goin' and more power to ya! Generally, a man with most of his planets in Leo will find a man who is "mostly" Virgo quite annoying . . . a real "antiromantic." And a heavy Virgo type will find a man with strong Leo planets to be just plain dumb. But if there is a serious chemical spark between them, chances are one or both have Venus or Mars in the other's Sun sign.

Their emotional issues (which we will get to) will come out and can get worked out in the bedroom. Mr. Leo loves the time that Mr. Virgo takes trying to please him. In fact *please* is too mild a word. The Leo man demands worship, and that is what he will get from his Virgo lover. And Mr. Virgo can't believe that a wretch such as him has earned the right to love someone as glamorous and wonderful as Mr. Leo.

Cut to a few years later. Mr. Virgo with the help of Mr. Leo has grown up and no longer has the low-self-esteem issues he had when he first hooked up with Mr. Leo. He may even *resent* that the relationship has been all about Mr. Leo and not enough about him (even though Mr. Virgo has insisted that it be that way).

Now comes the real test . . . can two emotionally healthy men, who love each other and happen to be born under the very different signs of Leo and Virgo, make a life together?

I believe they can if they can do this: wipe the slate clean and start anew. You see, the quality that both these men have in common is dedication. Let's say they belong to a political party. Perhaps that party votes in Joe Blowjob one year and four years later votes in Frank Fister. Each man will stick by his party and his new candidate. So what happens if while in a relationship Mr. Leo and Mr. Virgo both grow and evolve (which is what should happen, darlings). Can each man give a party cheer and a complementary fantastic fuck to the other and encourage each other to keep growing? Progress in their individuals lives should bring them together, not push them apart.

This relationship is so much about process it's hard to predict. But if they keep reassessing themselves and their feelings and talking about every nuance of emotion, they will remain dedicated to the ones they love: each other.

45.
Leo
and
Libra

The Leo man and the Libra man have one incredibly huge thing in common. Get your mind out of the gutter! The *huge* thing I am referring to is a gigantic, all-encompassing belief in *romance*. The old-fashioned kind that these days you can only find in a dog-eared and dusty book of sonnets or a New Orleans bordello. They may not always show it, but Leo men and Libra men believe in love in a most glamorous yet undeniably *girly* way. Both are full of paradoxes when it comes to love.

Let's start with Mr. Leo, who always enjoys going first. He is a strong, strong man who, when he gives his heart, gives it completely. He has a bit of the Samson-and-Delilah complex though, especially if he's been burned a handful of times. He wants to love completely, but he fears that if he gives it all up for one hot and soulful gentleman, then he will lose his strength, power, and maybe even his hair! That's why you can expect Mr. Leo to be just a little bit reserved and resistant during the initial period of amour. But once his walls come tumbling down, he's as true as they come.

Which brings us to Mr. Libra, who went to the rival school of love. The Libra man has quick reflexes in the romance department. When he senses that a man he meets (let's say a *Leo*, just for the hell of it) is love worthy, he will subtly but surely make sure that he does not let this guy walk on by. Mr. Libra will pour his heart out and worry about the consequences later. And believe me, he is quite sincere. It's *later* that he may feel overwhelmed by the intensity of his feelings, and even more so by the depth of his partner's feelings. At this point, he has only two choices: to fight for his own soul and the love that means the world to him, or to flee to figure it all out on his own in a quiet, safe place (like perhaps another man's arms).

I paint a dramatic picture, because both of these boys make love a number one priority in their lives, so the stakes are naturally very, very high.

Since the Leo seems to have more to risk here, what should he do? Well, after doing a serious background check on his potential Libra husband, which will entail hiring an astrologer, a private detective, and a go-go dancing brain surgeon named Beau (as a test), Mr. Leo must decide whether to leap or leave. And if he's in love already, he has no choice but to do the former.

The main piece of advice I have for these boys is to create a million different ways to keep the romance fresh and new. Yeah, yeah, yeah. Buy new sexy undies and butt plugs, check into a hotel for homos with a built-in dungeon under the Jacuzzi. What else?

Well, Mr. Leo should remember that Mr. Libra is an air sign, which means that intellectual stimulation means almost as much to him as anal stimulation does. (I said *almost.* Libra does rule the butt after all.) And Mr. Libra should not expect Mr. Leo to read his mind. Mr. Leo deals in big, broad strokes, so if you want him to take you to Brazil and dress you as Carmen Miranda when he fucks you, you'd better *tell* him. Your wish is his command.

And most of all, boys, remember not to fall into the trap that our hetero sisters and brothers fall victim to so often. Don't get so swept away in the planning of things—a big wedding, a new car, a trip to the Barbra Streisand Museum—that you forget to talk to each other and get to know each other. Don't use the art of romance to avoid one another, dear children. Use it to make your fantasies come true . . . together.

46.
Leo
and
Scorpio

What a powerful pair this is, boys and boys! Here we have another example of a couple in which both men's Sun signs square each other. Squares are challenging and present potential for growth and change for both fellows, but when we're dealing with fixed signs such as Leo and Scorpio, change does not come easily!

The attraction between them probably stems from the fact that although Scorpio is a water sign, it has many of the qualities of a fire sign. Co-ruled by the combative red planet, Mars, Scorpio can sometimes make big, tough, fiery Leo look like a pussy . . . cat that is.

The main trait these boys share is *loyalty*. The Scorpio man does not trust easily, but once he believes in you, that's it. Love never ends for him, unless it turns to hate, which is unlikely to happen while he's involved with a pure-of-heart type such as the Leo man. And Mr. Leo is as tried-and-true as they come. He will defend his Scorpio mate with a vengeance only once before seen, by Joan Collins on *Dynasty*.

Sexually, they make a hot pair. The Scorpio trusts the Leo in a way that allows him to let go of some control. Unlike most couples, whom I would advise to "talk more," for these boys I have two words (and, believe me, I had to edit them down from four): *shut up!* Loving can be incredible if they let their bodies do the talking, but the moment the Leo starts showing off—"You like that, don't you?"—or the Scorpio starts expressing his dark side in words— "This is gonna really hurt!"—laughter may be the response from the other, instead of passion. And we all know what laughter does to a big chubby. That's right. So less talking, more fucking please. And after the passions are sated, these guys have a cuddly camaraderie that is incredibly endearing.

The question for these boys, though, is not so much "Can they love each other?"—it's more, "Can they like each other?" Both should trust their instincts (and the advice of their closest companions) from the beginning. If the Scorpio man tells his friends, "I really like Mr. Leo, except for the fact that his reaction time to a clever remark is six point three hours, and he laughs at his own moronic jokes for twice that long," perhaps he should just listen to himself a little more carefully. And if the Leo man's friends see a cruel streak in the Scorpio man that the Leo is oblivious to, perhaps he should just trust his allies.

But if the other planets are groovy enough, and they can find enough in common besides good sex and a will to make their relationship work, then I say more power to them. And at that point, they will have more than enough power to set the world ablaze.

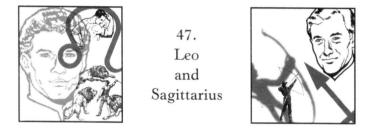

47.
Leo
and
Sagittarius

This pair of fire signs is likely to hit it off right away. The light-hearted and free-spirited Sag man can teach his Leo man a lot about having fun and forgetting about responsibilities, at least for a little while. These boys will have a great time playing together, whether it's on the soccer field, the dance floor, or the mattress. Both have a huge reserve of energy, enjoy the great outdoors, and love to live life at as loud a volume as possible. They are quite the bombastic pair!

These boys also really bring out the fire sign in each other. Chances are they will be on the go from the moment they hook up. The Sag man is certainly the more restless of the two, but the Leo man has been secretly waiting for an opportunity to explore the universe with a brave and reckless soul like Mr. Sag.

Sexually they are quite compatible. Mr. Leo is such a romantic that he brings the lovey-dovey side out of even the most cadike creature under the Sun (that's the Sag man). And Mr. Sag is so playful he can actually make his Leo mate forget about his useless pride and make him remember to just enjoy every crazy, kooky moment they have together. Sex between them is likely to be rambunctious and raw.

The danger for these boys is that they may burn out quickly. Even if they do, they are likely to remain pals to the end, but how *can* they make their love last? The key is in enjoying the quiet times.

You see, even though the Sag man is known around the globe as a "good-time Charlie," he does have his philosophical side. Usually, he spends most of his time running away from it, though. Mr. Leo can help his Sag lover to uncover his real dreams, not just his stupid schoolboy fantasies (okay, getting pissed on by a bunch of straight college boy wrestlers on top of Mount Everest *isn't* stupid. Are you happy now?).

Mr. Leo, on the other hand, needs constant attention and is rarely comfortable with solitude or traveling solo. The Sag man can show his Leo lover that independence is a good thing. Mr. Leo needs more freedom than he realizes, and he may find it in an open but secure relationship with a Sag.

Speaking of open, being faithful is not the Sag man's strong suit, and he'll be the first to admit it. But he can play by the rules if the rules have a lot of bend to them. These boys need to talk "monogamy" versus "nonmonogamy" early on in their union. Honesty is something they both value above most everything else, so there's no sense avoiding the inevitable relationship questions.

This is a most experiential relationship, full of constant questions and adventures. But the ride is bound to be fast moving, and always friendly.

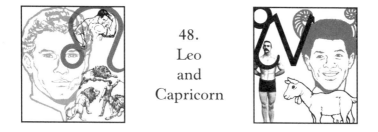

48.
Leo
and
Capricorn

These boys share a sense of pride and sense of snobbishness that seems like something out of a Henry James or Jane Austen novel. And both of those qualities are as transparent on them as a cheap skirt straight out of a Charles Busch theatrical romp. If they can both learn something from the least proud and least snobbish of all signs—Sagittarius—something called "laughing at one's self," then they could have a magnificent relationship together.

I bring up the sign Sagittarius because each has something in common with the nutty, irreverent centaur. Leo is a fire sign like Sag, and fire indicates warmth, openness, and a friendly nature. Mr. Leo should not forget this, even when his Capricorn is convincing him that a big bank account is more important that a big phone book filled with the numbers of good and dear friends. Mr. Leo can be foolishly snobbish and standoffish when life is treating him well. He must never forget that we are all human and equal (though, I admit, some of us more than others). And what does Cappy dear have in common with Sagittarius? Well, each Sun sign is supposed to learn something from the sign that precedes it. Sagittarius did not have adventure after adventure and learning experience after learning experience all over the world just so that his offspring, Capricorn, could put all those treasured reminders of the vastness of the world away in a shoe box in the closet. No, Mr. Capricorn must never forget the Sag lesson to keep his mind open and be ready to shake the hand of and learn something from every man or woman who crosses his path.

All that said, if these two boys can warm up a little and put asinine pride and social judgments toward the rest of world aside then they have the makings of a deliciously compatible and loving couple.

That said, let's talk about sex, shall we?

The chilly and reticent Capricorn man just loves to be warmed up by the his fiery Leo lover. While the Leo man, who isn't innately drawn to S/M, is somehow ravenously turned on by his Capricorn concubine's icy outer manner that masks an inner desire for daily degradation. In fact, both these boys are so *repressed* on a deep level that if one or even both are Catholic . . . forget about it! The sex is bound to be phenomenal once their real desires slowly rise to the surface.

And *slow* is the key word here. The Leo may be more revealing in an obvious way, but both men need a long time before they can really open up about their truest feelings. Once bonded, they are unusually protective of each other. This relationship, though, is definitely one where the body takes over late, late at night during their dark, sexual escapades. They have a secret club with only two members allowed in it. For two men who at first glance can be major snobs, there is a lot more tormented, sexy romance going on beneath the surface than either of them may ever realize.

49.
Leo
and
Aquarius

Certain signs are opposites and certain signs are *really* opposites. In the case of Mr. Leo and Mr. Aquarius, we are talking as opposite as, oh, I don't know, homo and hetero? That's right. And how can they meet in the middle? You guessed it. The dreaded and stupidly feared word: *bisexuality*. Oh, put your tongue back in your mouth, you silly queen. I don't mean that literally (although for some Leo and Aquarius pairs that may just do the trick). Let me explain.

Both these men were born under opposite fixed signs, which means they are both stubborn and opinionated but tend to stand on completely different sides of the fence. My guess is that at first meeting they will have some incredibly strong reaction to each other.

Most likely the Leo will be quite impressed by the Aquarius, who will not know that the Leo is alive. To make up for this initial brush-off, Mr. Leo will be sure to keep Mr. Aquarius at emotional arm's length later on.

Back to those opinions: if these two do get together, they will both find the most pleasure and the most frustration in arguing with each other about everything from the existence of a supreme being (and I don't mean you, Leo) to the merits of steaming broccoli rabe, versus sautéing. Oh, but can these girls argue! And as their relationship grows, each will find himself incredibly liberated when he begins to bend and let go of his rigid dogma once and for all, issue by issue.

That liberation of course only serves to heighten the ardor in the bedroom. And while we're in the boudoir, shall we go into detail? Oh, all right, let's! Sexually, these two make an unlikely but oh so unbelievable pair.

The Aquarius man loves to experiment and will take great pleasure in initiating the more conservative Leo into the territory that the great unwashed like to call kink. Mr. Leo is a creature of habit and a great believer in the pleasure principle, so once his kinky cherry is popped, this is the kind of reaction his Aquarius lover can expect from him: "Do it again, Jerry, and this time use the pineapple for a little longer. I want to really feel it." Mr. Aquarius may feel as if his sexual imagination has been co-opted and watered down, but I doubt he'll complain. No, he'll just lie back and enjoy it when his Leo lover decides to take charge and put all the electric toys and flavored fetish items away to simply ravish Mr. Aquarius the old-fashioned way. Man to man.

But can two divorced men share an apartment without driving each other crazy? Well, that's another story. But if you're wondering whether two men, one of the classic Leo persuasion and the other a thoroughly modern Millie of an Aquarius, can make it work over time, here's my answer:

Sure, baby! So long as they listen to Slick Jilly's rules of the road (tailor-made for this twosome):

- Respect your boyfriend's opinion, even when he is talking out of his ass.

- Do a regular check of your own rigidity (and I don't mean down there).
- And most importantly . . . always end an argument with some good sex. (If you can't shift from fighting to fucking, try this as a ploy: whoever comes last wins!)

Ah, if only Israel and Egypt could come to terms this way.

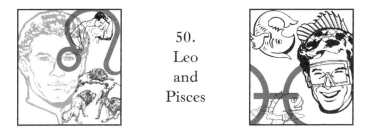

50.
Leo
and
Pisces

They seem to be from different planets, and they are. Mr. Leo is ruled by the Sun, which is big, bold, open, self-absorbed, warm, and loving. Mr. Pisces is ruled by Neptune, which is subtle, dark, dreamy, moody, sweet, and loving. Gee, I guess it's the fact that both have basically loving natures that brings them together. Go to the head of the class and give yourself a gold-star paddling just for fun!

Seriously, boys, Mr. Leo and Mr. Pisces could have a wonderful and whimsical, albeit bizarre, relationship, if they are so inclined. And whimsy is a big part of it. You see, Mr. Leo rules a house on the astrological wheel (the pizza-pie-shaped circle that charts are concocted on). He rules the fifth house, the house of big, Italian sausage. Whoops! I got carried away with the pizza analogy. Actually, the fifth house rules children. Whether the Leo man has children is up to him (his ex-wife, the adoption board, or his male lover's ingenuity), but there is no question that he is just a big child himself . . . and I mean that in the best possible sense. He is naive, yes, but he also has true faith in himself, the people he loves, and the world. Mr. Pisces, on the other hand, is ruled by Neptune, the planet of fantasy. Together, they could really spin some whimsical tales together.

And before we get too far away from fantasy, let's take a closer look at their sex life: lovemaking for them is apt to begin and end with a long, hot bath. Mr. Leo loves the luxury of it, and Mr. Pisces is swept away by the magic of his element: water. And between the pre- and postloving baths, what goes on? Perhaps a reenactment of another hot bath scene, let's say the one from *Spartacus* (from which the butt-boinking was sadly cut). Or perhaps a bedroom interlude that includes a bound Leo describing his dirtiest fantasies in coded words that only Mr. Pisces can understand. The Pisces man loves to serve and will be enamored with the idea of making his Leo lover's every dream come true.

So what happens after the deeds are done and these guys have called their Virgo houseboy over to clean the ring out of the tub? Well, other planets of course play a big part, but assuming those are pretty compatible, here's what to expect.

Mr. Pisces will feel divinely secure with Mr. Leo. The Leo man is the anchor that the Pisces man, who is sometimes too vague for his own good, really needs. Mr. Leo will adore being so adored by Mr. Pisces and will find the Pisces man mysterious and compelling, because, unlike Mr. Leo, he is so full of secrets. Or . . . they could live their fantasies out together while leading completely different inner lives.

So are they good for each other? It's a basic unanswerable question. Just as this question is: are our dreams real and our waking lives an illusion or vice versa?

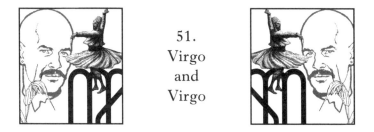

51.
Virgo
and
Virgo

Two Virgo men together? The word that comes to mind (after "Oy" of course) is *specific*. Virgo is ruled by Mercury, the quick-thinking and moving planet of the mind. And Virgo is the sign that rules details. Minutiae. The little things. If these two boys aren't too weirded out by the similarities they see or sense in each other to get together, then this is how I see the eccentric yet strangely erotic pairing of male Virgo with male Virgo.

First off, each has a secret life that he is completely open about. Most Virgo men are fine about admitting their various phobias and fantasies (and the two always overlap), usually on the first date. Once off to the bedroom (or more likely the bathroom or closet) to make love, that's where their compatibility will really be tested.

Both men like to take an experimental and surprisingly physical attitude toward sex. Yes, Virgos live in their head a lot (thinking, analyzing, thinking, analyzing . . . often compulsively), but they both think with their little heads, too! Virgo is an earth sign after all, which makes them . . . well, earthy!

Their sex life will undoubtedly be somewhat retro. They will regress to their pubescent days, when sex was really deviant! "I'll show you mine if you show me yours" is just the tip of the iceberg. These boys will want to reenact or transform every weird teenage experience that involved their dicks and give it a most grown-up spin.

So, after a romp in detention or a leisurely game of seven hours in heaven (they do have stamina . . . and patience), what then?

Well, the next test comes when the lease is signed and the boys are living together. Each Virgo man will move in complete with his own set of quirks, odd habits, and strange compulsions. Not all of this is bad, mind you. For instance, one of the Virgo men is likely to see food as love and could cook like a gourmet for his dear Virgo lover. The other Virgo man is likely to be superprotective and put on a butch role when dealing with rough homophobes out in the real world, and he will do everything in his power to stand up for his love and his lover. Do you see a certain dividing line between butch and femme, top and bottom, developing? It's there, you'll just have to get a closer look at the charts.

This nervous but rich union can last so long as each man finds the other's eccentricities endearing. Once that's established, these boys make wonderfully thoughtful lovers, companions, and pets! And they do well in pairs!

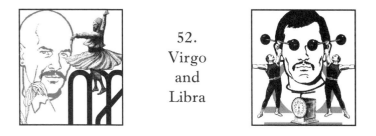

52.
Virgo
and
Libra

These two characters are both so cool, it may at first be hard to imagine either of them burning up with passion . . . let alone both of them crying out with sexual ecstasy, but stranger things have happened (see the previous section). Chances are they will be attracted to each other's mind first. Okay maybe not first, but *almost* first!

Both men are quite cerebral and analytical by nature and could easily get off on discussing everything from the mathematics of jazz improvisation to the pros and cons of celibacy (and you know where *that* discussion will ultimately end up!).

Once involved, these boys are loyal, loving, but strangely reserved. If the Virgo man has a healthy dose of Cancer in his chart, or the Libra man has a nice bit of Scorpio, then the fires of love may burn quite a bit hotter. Sexually, there is an underlying gentleness to this relationship. Oh, of course in the beginning one or both may want to show off what he's learned from this trick or that trick over the years. But once they have a groove going, there is something awfully sweet and quiet about their lovin'. And for two people who love to talk, they can say a lot more with their bodies than with their monologues when it comes to lovemaking.

The key to whether they can pull off this relationship is what they have in common, and their ability to keep teaching each other new stuff. The Libra man could open up the Virgo man's understanding about art (and life), and the Virgo man could easily improve the Libra's understanding of great literature and the details of modern filmmaking. This is definitely a relationship that will be made or broken in the details.

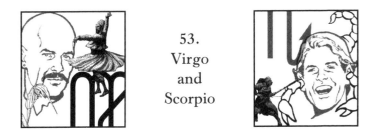

53.
Virgo
and
Scorpio

Both these men are intensely private people and are unlikely to share their true feelings easily. Yet, somehow, the "easy" sextile aspect between their signs makes it comfortable for these men to trust each other. Neither of them may say how he feels until some time has passed, but there is likely to be an instant feeling of camaraderie between these gents. The elements of a friendship are definitely there, but what about something a little more . . . passionate?

Well, the Scorpio man is apt to be surprised by the generally shy and quiet Virgo's interest in him . . . *in that way*. Mr. Virgo will pick up on Mr. Scorpio's intensity and sexiness almost immediately. Because the Virgo man at first appears so blasé, the Scorpio man is apt to flirt halfheartedly and then file Mr. Virgo under "Acquaintance. Probability of sex: unlikely." But after a few cigarettes, coffees, or beers (or all of the above) for courage, Mr. Virgo will probably be the one to ask Mr. Scorpio out.

Once the dating has begun, they will find communication smooth yet oddly *impersonal*. That's the Virgo man's influence. Talking about emotional things makes him nervous, especially when he's talking with a man he'd like to get down and dirty with. And speaking of down and dirty, it will no doubt be the Scorpio man who makes the first move, to move their relationship out of the realm of platonic or "unknown" and into the realm of "hot and heavy."

Sex between these guys is hot, and full of darkness and depth. The Scorpio man is turned on by the Virgo man's being such a complete nervous wreck. The Scorpio believes this a good sign. The Virgo man finds the Scorpio's directness to be a major plus. The Scorpio jumps right into sex and takes some of the responsibility off the Virgo man's shoulders (or other parts of his body).

At some point, though, the Virgo man is likely to freak out from the ambivalence he feels. It's in his nature to be nervous, and to freak out. The way the relationship goes from here depends on the Scorpio. If the Scorpio can take the Virgo man's feelings in stride and not pummel him with anger or anxiety, they can probably work through the trouble spots and grow quite comfortable and happy together. But if the Scorpio becomes reactive in the extreme, the Virgo man will probably pull further and further away, out of fear.

Fear is a major element in this union, but if these boys can help each other with their fears and obsessions—such as jealousy for the Scorpio man—they can make a great pair. Until they decide whether to be lovers or just friends, or even business associates, their relationship will seem like a poker game. Sexual heat, naturally, will be the wild card.

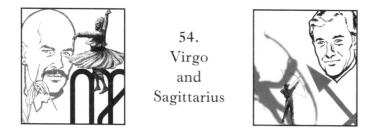

54. Virgo and Sagittarius

What could these two men possibly have in common? Good question! Actually, the first thing that comes to mind is "bodily functions" as in obsession with. These boys can laugh and talk for hours about gross aspects of the body and strange physical phenomena. Although the Virgo man may feign repulsion at the Sag man's scatological humor, he is actually quite turned on.

And therein lies the heart of their relationship: the physical. You see, these boys will immediately feel a physical attraction to each other and want to explore all the nooks and crannies of the other's body. Sex between them will probably be rough and full of laughs. The Virgo man will be relieved to find out that *nothing* horrifies his Sag lover. But he should also know that everything is fair game when it comes to kissing and telling. The Sag man doesn't realize (consciously) that he's horrifying Mr. V when he talks about the details of their fisting and enema sessions in front of Mr. V's family and friends at a wedding. Mr. Virgo, however, *will* be horrified (of course) when his embarrassing fetishes are revealed in public, and he'll be even madder when he sees how much all his pals and relatives adore Mr. Sag. And before you know it, the two men are knocking boots in the third pew as soon as the church is empty.

Sex is not the problem. It's everything else. These guys really do operate in totally different styles, but if their other planets make groovy aspects, they may be able to have a great relationship together. Chances are both men are drawn toward all things physical and may build a life together based on their love of nature, sports, and exploring the world . . . almost like two straight men who happen to enjoy butt-fucking and dancing for twelve hours at a circuit party! It would also help if they are both somewhat mature and share similar philosophies of life. Both signs do love to pontificate and argue "theory." If the sex is good enough and the level of mutual respect high enough, these boys could end up being the Siskel and Ebert of gay love.

55.
Virgo
and
Capricorn

These men, both earth signs, are naturally compatible. In a primal way, they speak the same language. Both men value security and believe in hard work. Mr. Virgo works for work's sake. He wants to feel useful and productive: to his lover, his boss, and the world. Mr. Capricorn is generally more ambitious and understands the value of strategizing and being persistent. These are the traits he will use to climb to the top in business, and to climb into the bed of Mr. Virgo.

Sexually, there will be probably be a lot of heat between these men. They are just so physically drawn together, and both will feel that they fit together in a most uncanny way . . . and in most uncanny positions! The Virgo man loves the Capricorn man's sadistic side, but should give back as good as he gets. After all, the Capricorn deserves some abuse, too!

Once together, these boys will find they have a lot in common. They enjoy the good things in life. As earth signs they appreciate the physical world in a most soulful way. Although both are probably somewhat workaholic, the time that they do spend together is bound to be sweet.

Mr. Capricorn, however, may grow tired of the Virgo's "humble" ways and could become of a bit of a harpy, telling his Virgo lover "Demand a raise!" or "Get a nicer car!" Mr. Virgo does have an appreciation for the simple things that Mr. Capricorn does not. Mr. V could become annoyed by his Capricorn lover's obsession with material success and wealth.

If their sex life stays a priority, though, I suspect they will be able to work out these conflicts. Both tend to withdraw and become cold and businesslike when they feel insecure, so they will have to make a real effort to keep the lines of communication open. And in the boudoir, Mr. Virgo and Mr. Capricorn must be careful not to become complacent with each other. They are likely to always have between B and B+ sex, but should keep striving for the big A+.

These men have a strong chance for lasting happiness together, mainly because they want the same things out of life. And earth signs (unless they have big Uranus problems) are unlikely to make drastic changes in their life's direction. Each should strive to grow, and with a little luck and lots of good sex they should find themselves growing and thriving together.

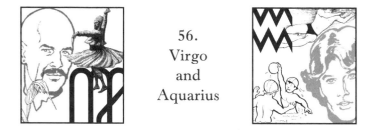

56.
Virgo
and
Aquarius

The word that comes to mind for this combination is *theoretical*. Both these men are cerebral and experimental and will wonder, "What would it be like to sleep with *him*? Why wonder? They will probably fall into bed quite easily, and sexually, they could be quite compatible. Mr. Aquarius will sense that Mr. Virgo likes to work, and to take orders. Being the more dominant personality, Mr. A, if he's smart (and most Aquarians certainly are), will train his Virgo lover to please him. Mr. Virgo has the biggest orgasms in bed and *(theoretically)* in life, when he gets the job done right. So the more he pleases the Aquarius man, the more satisfied he'll be.

But what about after the sheets are washed (by Mr. Virgo of course) and the lovemaking is over? What happens then? Well, it would help if they have a common line of work or passion about changing the world. Both men do desire to serve mankind in some way (and if they're both sexually compulsive, they may be able to do that literally!). Perhaps they both share a love of science or medicine and want to find a cure for AIDS, or a true understanding of the genetics of homosexuality (the "Mary" gene, I believe it's called). Their obsessions could certainly bring them together and keep them together.

But their styles, I must tell you, are wildly different. Mr. Virgo is a fanatic for details, while Mr. Aquarius likes to think *and* act globally. They may complement each other well or they may annoy the hell out of each other or both. Of course, in a case like this when two signs are inconjunct to each other—an odd combination to begin with—a lot will depend on the other planets. If the Aquarius has moon in Pisces or Virgo rising, that would help. It would also be grand if the Virgo man has moon in Aquarius or Leo rising.

The real challenge for this couple will be to find some emotional middle ground . . . or any emotion at all! They do make a chilly pair. Oh, sure, the Virgo's nervous nature could be construed as being emotional, but crying because he's out of vermouth doesn't count. The Aquarius of course wrote his dissertation on intellectualizing, so you can imagine the warmth these two stir up.

Heavy water-sign planets help, and so does a real effort to develop intimacy. Chances are, though, that a crisis will make or break this relationship. Both click into a more feeling and compassionate mode in an emergency. Then, of course, the temptation will be to create crises in order to achieve closeness. Self-reflection will help more than words can say or theories can explain.

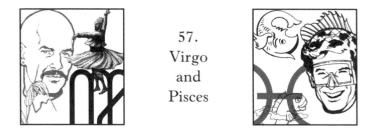

57.
Virgo
and
Pisces

These quirky gentlemen, born under opposite mutable signs, usually make a fine pair. They balance each other out in a "yin-yang" way (even though both have often been called and often think of themselves as "pussy boys"). Still, pretty early in the relationship, one of them will undoubtedly fall into a top role while the other takes the bottom. The strongest connection these men have is that both are truly nurturing people. The Pisces nurtures in an emotional way. Ruled by Neptune, the planet of illusion, Mr. Pisces nurtures with his imaginative and often magical gift of healing. He will dig deep to understand his Virgo lover and will shower him with love, affection, and empathy, unconditionally. Mr. Virgo is more practical but is just as sincere in his desire to serve the man he loves. His way of showing it may be to organize his Pisces lover's closet or to organize an on-line banking system for him. Ain't love grand?

Actually, this relationship has a depth that both these men will probably feel right away. They bring out each other's serious side. And that seriousness comes through in bed. The emotional intensity that lies just beneath the surface in this relationship will come through in a big way when these guys get it on.

The catch is, this relationship could turn out to feel *too* heavy at times for both of them. And that will come through in the sack, as well as in other areas. The Pisces man, for instance, does have a playful, silly, and downright ridiculous side, which the Virgo man patronizingly indulges, but probably doesn't *truly* understand or appreciate. Only the Pisces man's friends or (gulp) exes really dig his wild side. The Virgo man is more intent on making an honest woman . . . er, man of his Pisces lover.

On the flip side, the Virgo man has lots of funky fetishes that he really doesn't like to share. The Pisces man can be a wee bit pre-

sumptuous and may try to get overinvolved in the Virgo man's id-
iosyncrasies, when the Virgo man just wants to go about his business
and not feel emotionally invaded. Mr. Pisces may not ever realize
how truly self-conscious his Virgo lover is.

But, all in all, they do have a lot of potential as long-term lovers.
Hopefully one or both of them have strong fixed (Taurus, Leo, Scorpio, or Aquarius) signs in their chart. That will add some backbone
and staying power to this union. Mutual friends also add strength
to their relationship, because they *both* will benefit from frequent
reality checks. The pal who advises Mr. Pisces, "Tell him to stop
alphabetizing your hair products," and the friend who points out to
Mr. Virgo, "Your boyfriend should never drink more than one Long
Island iced tea," are the ones who will really help keep this relationship alive and thriving. Without friends like that, Mr. Pisces
will be too vague and Mr. Virgo will be too fixated on the little
things to be able to communicate successfully with each other. They
both need coaches.

·58.
Libra
and
Libra

These boys make a rather sweet couple. And I mean sweet as in
four double-chocolate cupcakes with two black-and-white milk-
shake chasers. They can really go over the top, because both guys
love to say, "I have a boyfriend!" "Isn't he cute?" "Oh, I just love
my lover-honey!" Yeech! Diabetics stay away. This much sugar
could kill you. But they could be very happy in their own little
lovey-wuvvy-cutesy-wutesy little world.

They definitely share a similar temperament. Both these men like
to chill out and be mellow. Their real idea of fun is to go out to eat,
go to a show, come home and do it, and then fall asleep while
listening to Roxy Music (Mr. Mod, Bryan Ferry, is a Libra, too,

you know). Sounds pretty wonderful, doesn't it? And when times are good, they are really good.

It's when problems arise that the relationship is really tested. Neither of these boys particularly likes to *work*. They love just going along and enjoying each other's company. But when the time comes when one discovers that his *honey bunny sweetie baby* has a cruel streak or when the other shows his claws in a calculatingly cold way during their first argument, well, I promise you, darling, the fur *will* fly.

If they can manage to get through their fights without fucking other people for revenge, or emotionally straying to a high degree (e.g., fantasizing about the butcher's son daily), then they are probably adult enough to have a truly magnificent love affair. But I warn you, neither man is too crazy about dealing with the tough realities of long-term love.

Sexually, they can be quite the dynamic duo, especially if they have the right props. Both can be a little on the dreamy side, so it helps if they have the right accoutrements: the right butt plug, cockring, champagne, and chocolate. Both like sex to be easy and luxurious.

Aesthetic pleasure is also key in this relationship. Both Libra men need to be surrounded by beauty, so if they can keep themselves looking lovely and can put some energy into decorating a beautiful home together, that should help, or else eyes may wander to the godlike Greek who works as a trainer at the local whorehouse . . . I mean, gym.

The key to long-term happiness for these men lies in the simplest but must challenging word: *commitment*. That means vowing to stick by each other through bad times and good, and to put some elbow grease into making this relationship work. It also means putting in some extra effort to understand the other in a meaningful way, even during pooky-wooky-schweetie happy times.

59.
Libra
and
Scorpio

This combination is chock-full of possibilities, but I must warn you, these boys could bring out each other's *bad* side. In bed, that's a good thing of course. The sexual attraction will be the first thing that clicks for these boys. There is a certain "opposites attract" quality to this combination—even though they are not opposite signs—because Mr. Libra is ruled by peace-loving Venus while Mr. Scorpio is co-ruled by battle-ready Mars. The Libra man will work his way into the Scorpio's heart through the back door (get your mind out of the gutter!). He will take the gentle and coy approach and will do his best to subliminally force the Scorpio man to obsess about him. The more aggressive Scorpio will make the first move and think it's all his idea. Ha!

Once together, sex happens quickly, and it is likely to be hot, hot, hot. Two things will be happening simultaneously. The first is their mutual desire to dazzle the other. The Libra man will want to impress his Scorpio lover with his beauty. Why else would he pose himself in just the perfect position in the most flattering light? The Scorpio man will use his volcanic sexual intensity to woo Mr. Libra. The other thing going on is less plotted (yes, both these boys are naturally manipulative), and that thing is called love.

These guys are likely to get infatuated with each other quickly. It may be love, it may be infatuation. Only time will tell them which it is. But both of them could easily slip into a passionate affair because they each believe the other possesses something he needs. Mr. Scorpio believes subconsciously, that Mr. Libra can bring balance and harmony to his life. Clichéd? Yes. But that's how he feels. Mr. Libra is drawn to the Scorpio man because of his power and strength. He believes this could be the man he can lean on emotionally; the man who can protect him.

Corny? Yes. Horny? Yes, they are. It's a combination that means *something* has to come of this union, and they'd better decide early what that's gonna be.

It could just be an affair. After all, during the hours when they are not under each other's sexual spell, they may both realize that it is just a sexy, mysterious thing between them, nothing that could last in the "real world." Or it could be love. And with love comes a commitment to stand together, against the world, in an unbreakable union of two. Before they go out and buy rings, though, they should spend the four seasons together. See how they deal with life's ups and downs. Do they complement each other or offend each other's sensibilities? They must be extremely honest with each other and with themselves. The Scorpio could idealize the Libra and vice versa. They may be too charming, in their different ways, for their own good. Their real natures must be addressed. If they (consciously or unconsciously) hide their "dark" sides from each other, then the third possibility for these men is to become bitter enemies once the truth comes out. Cut to the chase, boys!

60.
Libra
and
Sagittarius

This is a naturally compatible combination because each man's Sun sign makes a smooth and groovy sextile aspect to the other. Mr. Libra and Mr. Sagittarius could hit it off right away. They are both sociable and lighthearted and have a somewhat adolescent attitude toward romance. Oh. Sorry, boys. I guess my acerbic Scorpio tongue and my tactless Sag rising are showing. I don't mean to suggest that these guys are immature lovers. They are just both a little selectively oblivious. Oops. There I go again . . . insulting you guys! Well, I guess that helps me to make a ham-handed segue into my next point about the way that they are most different: communication styles. You see, Mr. Libra was born under the sign of diplomacy and always likes to put a little sugar on top of whatever he has to say and tends to communicate in a most roundabout fashion. For instance, if he thinks his Sag lover is wearing a tacky shirt, he might say, "Take off that shirt so I can see your body." Would you even guess that he is doing his damnedest to *not* puke over the Sag's fringe cowboy frock? The Sag, on the other hand, will say the most inappropriate, embarrassing things without even realizing it. If his Libra lover was wearing something he didn't like, he might just blurt out, "Wow, those pants make your thighs look huge and your basket look tiny!" And unlike a stinging Scorpio, Mr. Sag truly means no harm. But who cares? His Libra lover just wants him to shut up! They should both take a look at the influence of Mercury (the planet of communication) in their charts, in relation to each other.

Aside from this bone of contention, this has the potential to be a really fun and wonderful relationship. The Sag man's sunny and optimistic personality really brings out the best in his Libra lover, who is often too embarrassed to admit that he sees the world through rose-colored glasses. Mr. Sag will let him know that it's okay to be the big, goofy dreamer he is. And Mr. Libra will provide Mr. Sag with the consistency that he so desperately needs. The Sag man loves to wander and roam the world (even if it's just in his mind), but it will warm his heart in a deep and spiritual way to know that he is truly loved by his Libra man.

Of course, with love comes the question where do we go from here? Mr. Libra is the marrying kind and Mr. Sag has a more rambunctious and rambling romantic nature (thus the cowboy shirt). These fellows will have a long way to go before deciding on whether to tie the knot or just tie each other up and have fun . . . perhaps for years. And speaking of tying up, their sex life is bound to be playful and exciting. They have a strong friendship aspect between them, too, which may dilute the passion from time to time, but chances are a major night (or month) of soul-searching between them will bring the intensity back.

There's only one real, significant danger for this couple. I'll give you a hint: Nancy Sinatra recorded a song about it in the sixties and the Thompson Twins recorded a song on the same subject in the eighties. For you idiots who are thinking, "Hold My Boots Now," or something equally ridiculous, why don't I just tell you the answer? "Lies." (That's the Nancy S song.) That's right. "Lies. Lies. Lies." (That's the Thompson Twins, darling.) Both these boys tend to be a little bit less than completely honest. It's a lifelong challenge actually. They are just both more prone to taking the easy way out of most situations, so the truth can be just a little too much work for a little too little *immediate* payoff. If they're going to try to make it work over the long term, they'd better deal with this issue head-on. No lie.

61.
Libra
and
Capricorn

This is another example of a "square" relationship. I refer to the astrological "square" that tends to create friction between two signs, but in this case it could be the other kind of "square," too. They do tend to bring out the cautious and conservative sides of each other. The Capricorn man has an innate need for respectability, while the Libra man is a fool for luxury. Together that spells *bourgeois*. If these two boys can admit that they value the simple, traditional, and *expensive* things in life, then they could be happy together. Yet, somehow, seeing their materialistic desires (Capricorn) and pleasure-principle nature (Libra) reflected in the other's eyes may make these boys uncomfortable with each other.

That discomfort could lead to avoidance or to getting to know each other better. Chances are they'll be chilly rivals first, then hot sex partners, and then . . . well, we've already got a glimpse of the chill, so let's get to the hot-sex part next. The Capricorn man, who is so disciplined and never let's himself get away with *anything,* will surely think the Libra man is a big, spoiled brat and will punish him accordingly. In addition to whipping the Libra's bubble butt, Mr. Capricorn will also deny Mr. Libra all the delicious things he desires. This teasing and torturing can drive them both crazy for hours. And Mr. Capricorn will also dig giving his Libra lover orders and making him work. Work: the most important element of the Capricorn man's life, and the concept the Libra man does his best to avoid.

Besides having some incredibly racy times in the boudoir, these fellows will also enjoying debating and testing each other's mental prowess. Mr. Libra tends to put more value on aesthetics, while Mr. Capricorn is interested in the material worth of things: from a convertible Mercedes to his own mother. Luxury-loving Libra and practical Capricorn should have a lot to argue about.

The question remains, what then? These boys will certainly have to have a lot of compatible aspects in their charts to really build a relationship together. But assuming they do, the challenge of their Sun-sign combination is to find a way to respect each other's differences and remain turned on by them.

62.
Libra
and
Aquarius

These air-sign boys certainly have the ability to get along well and are incredibly compatible on many levels. The main trait they have in common is their braininess. Mr. L and Mr. A are both clever, great thinkers. The Aquarius man is constantly thinking about the world at large and his place in it. He enjoys freedom, but even if he only gets to travel once in a while, he can still experience all the freedom he desires through his mind. Mr. Libra is focused on the meaning of partnership. He can see the world more clearly when he bounces his well-constructed arguments off another person. Mr. Libra will enjoy being challenged by his Aquarius lover because he trusts him and can appreciate the Aquarian's desire to be objective and fair. The Libra man has the same desire. These men can be so potentially simpatico that they have to be careful not to fall into a simple friendship, where sex and romance take a backseat to scintillating intellectual discussions.

What happens in the bedroom will determine a lot.

Sexually, these fellows are certainly in sync and can easily get into a romantic groove together. The Libra man knows how to set the scene and bring out the sensual side of the sometimes frosty Aquarius. The Libra will light candles that drip nice thick wax, play some suggestive music with a deep, sultry groove, and slip into some sexy, slutty underwear, all to lead the Aquarius man into a place of heavenly delights. The Aquarius, meanwhile, lives to experiment sexually and will sense early on that the Libra man is ready, willing, and able to do almost anything in bed, no matter how shocking or wild . . . as long as Mr. Libra can lie on his back to do it (he hates to "over"-use his physical energy). Anyway, all of this is grand, but there could be a slightly detached feeling to their lovemaking. If real love can come through as they are fucking the shit out of each other, than I have real, high hopes for these boys. If they are just playing a highly stylized game of "I'll show you mine if you show me yours," then the relationship will probably turn buddy-buddy sooner than not.

If that real love is there, I promise you this: it will run deep, much to the surprise of both of these cool characters. Their relationship could take on a brotherly soul-mate quality. Their commitment to each other could be profound. Which doesn't mean they won't sleep with other people, because . . . well . . . let's just say they both have their reasons. Mr. Libra is supremely sensual and Mr. Aquarius is supremely nonmonogamous. This is an issue they should definitely discuss in depth, though, before exchanging rings.

63.
Libra
and
Pisces

These two fellows together are the height of mellow. Once they get into bed together, they are unlikely to get out, unless the remote breaks or the neighborhood restaurants stop delivering takeout. It's just their way. They like to relax. These guys do bring out the gentle side in one another, too. The Pisces man is so empathetic he hates to hurt a fly, and he's certainly going to make every attempt to be sweet to his lovable Libran lover. The Libra, in turn, is so diplomatic, he will find just the right words to say to his Pisces lover when a difficult situation arises.

The problem, as you may already see, between the two sides of this astrological inconjunct relationship is this: Where's the energy? Their relationship could be so low-key that it barely has a pulse. And the most likely way that these chaps could infuse their union with some drive is by using illicit substances. This relationship could be a bizarre love triangle, between Mr. Libra, Mr. Pisces, and their *dolls*. Mr. Pisces, of course, was born under the sign that personifies drug use. Factor in years of abuse at the hands of a homophobic society (and probably family and youthful peer group), and I smell an alcoholic blackout. Now, for those Pisces who are overly addicted (or addicted to men who are addicted), they know what they have to do, although it's the hardest thing in the world. These gentle Pisces men need to give up the devil on their shoulder and get clean. Mr. Libra, unfortunately, can be a bad, bad influence. He likes to push the boundaries of "moderation" and decadence and could pull Mr. Pisces into a deep, dark place.

The thing these guys have to do is find another way to get high together. And the best way I can think of is by fucking each other's brains out regularly. In bed, you see, they really do have a fierce connection (besides their love of pay-per-view movies). They are slow moving, slow to come, and ever so hot, in an indulgent "let's make this last as long as we can" kind of way.

If the Libra man and the Pisces man can always keep an eye out for the bad influences of active addiction (and the deceit that goes with it), they can enjoy all the wonderful experiences they are meant to have together.

64.
Scorpio
and
Scorpio

Two Scorpio men together could set the world on fire or set each other on fire . . . literally! These boys have strong passions and appetites and could devour each other with lust and love or destroy each other with torment and cruelty. They will probably have a strong vibe right away. They could size each other up and become good friends—not *best* friends, though, they're both too high maintenance. They will probably recognize themselves in each other, and if the similarities are too strong, there may not be a major attraction. It's not self-loathing, it's self-*knowing*, darling. They know how much energy and attention they need and may not *want* a powerhouse of a Scorpio boyfriend to compete with them. Or there might be just the right chemistry to pull them together with an electric kind of magnetism that nobody could stand in the way of.

Sex between these men is hot, hot, hot . . . if there is a glimmer of trust, that is. Without that assurance then it just becomes a battle of "Who's hotter?" Ho-hum. Assuming that there is an emotional draw between them, sex can be life-altering. Both Scorpio men like to get deep into the heart of the other's soul and body. Sex is a long, orgasmic dance with the devil, and when it's over, both will feel purged . . . for five minutes, and then it's time to get going again.

While they are still at the pure lust level, they are still safe. It's when love appears on the scene that things get really dangerous. You see, both men are jealous, possessive, and volatile. So when the fur flies, it really flies, say for instance if one of them dares to flirt with (or be courted by) another man. Each Scorpio wants to own the other, which may be fine . . . in theory. But from time to time, each of these fiery water-sign men is going to want to show some independence.

It's a delicate balance they've got to keep together, but passion will never be a problem. Not killing each other, however, could be.

65.
Scorpio
and
Sagittarius

Talk about two wild cards! These boys both have a spark of unpredictability and a draw toward danger. Together, they tend to bring out the risk-taker in each other. The Scorpio man is more controlled and less obvious about his desire to walk on the wild side, while the Sag man is loud and raucous and let's the whole world know that he's looking for trouble.

Chances are, these boys will meet in a social setting, probably one that involves dancing, drinking, and cheap feels. The Sag will probably make the first move on the Scorp. He's the more physically free and will tend to take a "what the hell" attitude toward coming on to Mr. Scorp. After all, if things don't work out, Mr. Sag can do his favorite thing: move on. But Mr. Scorpio is a serious man. He may be a good-time Charlie, too, as the Sag man certainly is, but he doesn't play around emotionally.

So once these boys start dating, Mr. Scorpio will hold Mr. Sag to some pretty high standards. The Sag man may actually like having to live up to someone else's expectations. It could be a new and positive experience for him. And who better to try to please than his hot new lover.

And sex between them could be pretty hot. Mr. Sag may be surprised by how much he *feels* when he's getting it on with Mr. Scorp. The Scorpio man knows that his Sag lover is drawn to him passionately, and this will only make the Scorpio man more enamored. But the Sag fellow is likely to get scared by the intensity of this relationship. After all, he is a free spirit and absolutely *hates* to feel tied down. Plus, their basic natures—Scorp's so serious and driven and Sag's so light and free-spirited—aren't exactly compatible.

But this relationship can work, if there are a few important, mitigating factors in place. If the Sagittarius has a significant amount of water or earth in his chart, he may be more likely to want to stick around and enjoy the heaviness of a relationship with a Scorp. Or if the Scorpio has a lot of fire and air in his chart and is more flexible and less possessive than your average Scorpio man, he may be more open to letting the relationship develop in a natural and easy way. Also, if these boys have lived a little bit and know what they want and decide they've got a shot, nothing can put out the fire of their passion.

66.
Scorpio
and
Capricorn

The Scorpio man and the Capricorn man have similar MOs. Both men are driven, goal-oriented, serious people who beneath the surface possess a volcanic passion for sex and life. The Scorpio man may be more attention grabbing and the Capricorn man may be more of a "regular guy," but these are just their surface personas. The exciting thing is that once these boys slip into something more comfortable and start their sexual escapades, an intimate kind of intensity develops right away. They may both be shocked by the power of their sexual passion for each other.

The Scorpio will probably be the one to hunt down the Capricorn, in a back-door way, of course. You see, the one area where they differ is in that Mr. Scorpio is ruled by his curiosity and is compelled to open "Pandora's box" (even, and I suppose especially, if Pandora is a guy), while Mr. Capricorn is safe and cautious and lives perfectly well without knowing firsthand the passion that lurks beneath the surface in his friendship with Mr. Scorpio.

I mention friendship because these two men, whose Sun signs make a pleasant, sweet sextile to each other, have the potential to be great friends and/or colleagues. Mr. Capricorn will probably be attracted to Mr. Scorpio right away but may (sensing the reckless side of Mr. Scorpio) steer their relationship in a less loaded direction. Since both men are obsessive about their work, Mr. Capricorn may suggest that they partner up in business. Mr. Scorpio will probably push the boundaries of what's appropriate to find out for sure what could be.

Sexually, the bond between them is strong. They both are relentless and driven in bed and will stop at nothing to please each other and themselves. Sex is definitely heated. Mr. Scorpio will be incredibly excited by Mr. Capricorn's earthy *realness*. The Capricorn will find his never-endingly mysterious Scorpio lover intriguing and sexy beyond belief.

The main challenge for these boys after the lovin' is this: What are they each looking for? Both are so goal-oriented in life that if either senses that they will eventually go in different directions, he is likely to pull back and nip the relationship in the bud. And in truth, one is likely to scare more easily than the other in this combination, though which one is likely to spook first is hard to say. Perhaps neither will, if their lives are in sync. But for this combination, the question "Do we know where we're going to?" will be superimportant. A casual relationship is just not in the stars for them. It's all or nothing at all, kiddies.

67.
Scorpio
and
Aquarius

This combination either clicks or doesn't. These boys are from two different planets, Scorpio being from intense, personal, and volatile Pluto, and Aquarius being from controversial, cerebral, and innovative Uranus. They are fixed people whose Sun signs make a difficult square to each other. On the surface, both may be too stubborn and set in their ways and just plain *different* to really make a strong effort to pursue each other. The transiting stars will have to be on their side to make the timing just right.

If they do get under each other's skin, then they are likely to get in each other's pants soon enough. Sexually, they make a bizarre and sometimes amazing combination. The Scorpio man is likely to be extrasensual with the Aquarius man, who tends to have a more abrupt (Uranian) sexual style. Mr. Scorpio may slow the pace down, to keep the heat simmering. Mr. Aquarius is likely to want to explore all the different possibilities for pleasure with his Scorpio lover. These men are both searching for the ultimate orgasm (Scorpio) and the ultimate and untried path to it (Aquarius).

After the postcoital cigarettes, though, what then?

Well, this relationship is apt to be filled with contradictions. The good thing about these guys is that if they like each other, they are likely to become fiercely loyal to each other and protective of one another right away. They can rely on each other. However, when they are alone, communication could be a challenge, unless they have a bunch of other planets that are compatible. The Scorpio man is driven by his emotions, and what's in his gut, while the Aquarius man is ruled by his logic. The fascinating part of this combination will be in the attempts each man makes to understand the other. Both like a challenge, and, boy, will this be the challenge of a lifetime!

The key to this odd combo's success will be a common passion . . . be it music, science, or crime. Both are the obsessive type, so if they can share their obsessions with each other, they have an excellent chance at a relationship. Still, it's bound to be a bit of a bumpy road, since their signs don't tend to blend smoothly together. Both boys will have to learn to compromise and grow a little. They can learn a lot from each other. Mr. Aquarius could learn to deal with his feelings more, while Mr. Scorpio can learn to stop taking everything so personally. Trust deepens over time with these two, also. It could take years for them to achieve the real intimacy they are capable of together.

Monogamy will be another interesting issue for them to grapple with. The Aquarius by nature is the symbol of *non*monogamy, while Mr. Scorpio is the most jealous and possessive man in the zodiac.

Interesting already, isn't it? They should be as honest as possible about this issue and experiment with what's comfortable. They may come up with a bizarre set of rules that works well for them, and that their friends shouldn't even *try* to comprehend. Hey, if their rules are "you can get a blow job from a man in uniform every other Friday, but anything else is considered *cheating,*" well . . . whatever! These men are innovative and brilliant, so maybe they're on to something. Who are we to judge?

68.
Scorpio
and
Pisces

These water-sign men certainly seem to be compatible. They are both emotional, intuitive, and mysterious . . . to themselves as well as to each other. The Scorpio man has a more fiery quality and will probably be the one to push for a romance. Mr. Pisces tends to be a "go with the flow" type who is easily influenced by the strong Scorpio. But before he knows it, the impressionable Pisces man will be caught up in the intense world of Mr. Scorpio. Mr. Scorpio has a turbulent nature, but Mr. Pisces knows how to gently calm his volatile lover. Mr. Pisces on the other hand is sometimes vague and passive when it comes to taking charge of his life. The Scorpio man will have a good influence on him in this way. Mr. Scorpio is so driven and focused, he will have no problem giving his Pisces man a little career counseling followed by a night of passion.

Both men have to be careful when it comes to substance use, as they both have a proclivity for addiction. If the only time they have sex is when they are totally high, they should ask themselves why. These boys could be a great influence on each other or a horrible one. So long as both men have the other's best interests at heart, they can help each other to break some destructive habits and cross over into a place of true happiness and success. Or they could lead each other to the darkest, most dangerous place either of them has ever visited. This duo is incredibly powerful together.

In bed, they have the potential to drive each other wild, so long as the Scorpio softens up his sometimes controlling style, and the Pisces puts some energy into his lovemaking. When it's hot, it's hot. Both men are sensual and imaginative. Role-playing brings out the best in them; these guys have such active fantasy lives, it would be a shame if they didn't act out together some of their favorite scenes. Even though Mr. Scorpio is the more dominant one, he will totally dig being restrained and overwhelmed by his Pisces lover. In bed, Mr. Pisces can certainly butch up to please the demanding Mr. Scorpio.

As their relationship deepens, their sex life will be a direct reflection of their happiness together. When communication is off, or when needs aren't being met, the first place the truth will come out will be in bed.

Provided these boys open up to each other continually (they are both secretive by nature) and are careful around anything that is addictive (from booze to hustlers), they could have a beautiful relationship.

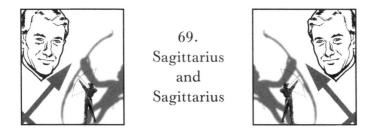

**69.
Sagittarius
and
Sagittarius**

These boys could be soul mates who understand each other in a deep, karmic way, or they could each be the one to turn the other to a life of crime and debauchery. Two Sag men together make a strong, fiery combination. Have you ever had sushi and accidentally eaten too much wasabi? Try doubling that effect and you'll have an idea what these boys are like together.

There is no doubt that they can have fun together. Sagittarian men like to party, and even the ones who have sworn off "party favors" still like to stay up all night and talk, dance, eat, and fuck (in no particular order, and often all at once). In each other, they could find their match: someone who is garrulous, roguish, and optimistic.

In bed, they make quite a wild duo. Each man's goal may be to outshock the other. They may end up shocking the neighbors instead. These boys are bawdy, loud, and incorrigible and love doing what they're not supposed to do. If one Sag tells the other he's really into bondage but *hates* wearing a blindfold—it freaks him out—guess what? The other Sag will push the boundaries just a little to see if his lover will go further with him than with anyone else before. Challenges. They both love them.

The danger here is that the relationship could burn out just as easily as it begins. These guys could be just too much alike. After all, somebody has to take care of the laundry and grocery shopping, and it ain't gonna be either of these Sag men.

70.
Sagittarius
and
Capricorn

There is something distinctively hot about this combination. Chances are, if they are very drawn to each other, one of them probably has Venus in the other one's Sun sign (which is often the case when two people's birthdays fall within weeks of each other). One or both of them may feel as if he's found his fantasy lover.

Sexually, they can be very compatible. The Capricorn man is the king of saying no and turning down the room temperature to freezing. Mr. Sag sees his Capricorn lover's rigid nature—"I have to work," "This isn't the right time or place"—as a challenge. And Mr. Capricorn loves a forceful lover. After holding it together and being so sober and hardworking by day, Mr. C will relish breaking every taboo with his Sag lover by night.

Fantasy is very different from real life, however, and how these boys lead their real lives couldn't be more contrary. Most Sag men are terribly irresponsible and terribly charming (which is how they get away with all their nonsense). But Mr. Capricorn is a puritan at heart, with a strong work ethic, who may find the Sagittarian man's lifestyle distasteful. After a while, he will demand that Mr. Sag shape up or ship out. Mr. Sag could get a real job and a real direction in life, but is that really his way? At heart this fire-sign man is more of a wanderer and a searcher, and too much time with the stoic and pensive Capricorn man could put his fire out.

The ideal scenario is possible but takes a major adjustment on both their parts. The Capricorn man may have to loosen up a bit and stop clinging so desperately to his suffocating rule system. If he does take a leaf from his Sag lover's book and starts living life one wild and crazy moment at a time, he may actually end up being more successful (his ultimate desire) than he ever dreamed of. His options could open up considerably (for example, if he runs off for a wild week in the Bahamas with Mr. Sag, he may end up sipping piña coladas with a financial mogul who takes him under his wing), and he will certainly enjoy life more. And Mr. Sag could learn a lesson or two from Mr. Capricorn about how to stop chasing his tail, and actually start living up to his ideals and dreams. The Sagittarius man tends to spread his energy (and his seed) all over town, and in the end he may not get anywhere. The earth-sign man can teach the fire-sign man how to *focus*.

For this relationship to work, both men will have to write the rule book and then make an honorable attempt to stick to it.

71.
Sagittarius
and
Aquarius

These fellows make a most *outrageous* combination. The main thing they have in common is their exhibitionism. Oy, do these boys love to get naked in front of large crowds. Nudism is a way of life for them. If you enjoy dancing, why not do it sans garb and enjoy it that much more? The same philosophy holds true for going to the movies and taking the bar exam. Clothes are just so *inhibiting,* aren't they? And this love of showing their bodies is really just symbolic for their mutual love of freedom . . . at any price. Of course, it's the rest of us who pay the price, when we just want to enjoy a nice lesbian picnic in Prospect Park without having to watch these lads rub sunblock on each other's *private* parts.

So it's freedom that they both love, right? Well, how does one base a long-term relationship on a love of freedom? That's quite a GRE question, isn't it, dears? Well, since they are both naturally *non*monogamous, they should probably agree to an open relationship right off the bat. Living up to their ideal, though, can be tough going.

These guys may both be spawned from that rare breed of humans that is not jealous or possessive in any way. Even so, they may discover a type of emptiness that stems from a real lack of intimacy. These fellows both tend to avoid listening to their hearts and acting from their feelings first, rather than from their highfalutin philosophical constructs.

How they fare when they are alone together without a lot of outside stimuli will tell them the most about how they can deal over the long term. Oh, and how's the humping? Fabulous . . . but it's all for show.

72.
Sagittarius
and
Pisces

This combination is another example of a square aspect between Sun signs, and in this case the boys are ruled by opposite elements: fire and water. So what could possibly bring them together? I wish I knew. But if there is an attraction between them, there definitely is some hope. For one thing, both signs have a different but equally strong belief in fate. The Sag man, ruled by Jupiter, planet of good luck, has a deep and stupid belief that the wheel of fortune will spin in his favor. That's why he rarely takes responsibility for his actions! Mr. Pisces, ruled by the mystical planet Neptune, is constantly looking for signs and omens and has a basic fear of the universe. That's why he has such drug-addict tendencies and possesses a basic desire to hide from the punishing hand of fate. Together these two make the perfect combination of stupid optimism (Sag) and obsessive negativity (Pisces).

In bed, they can make magic together. No act is too humiliating for Mr. Pisces, and absolutely nothing fazes or embarrasses Mr. Sag. The lack of inhibition when their clothes come off is so significant, it embarrasses *me* just thinking about it. All right, I'll get over it. These men will unconsciously push each other's boundaries and delve into areas that are emotionally loaded. And I'm still talking about their sex life! This is deep stuff, although they may both be initially fooled into thinking it is just hot (and weird) sex. Memories of sexual abuse, which are so prevalent in our community, fear-of-intimacy issues, alcoholism, etc., are ripe to be exposed during one heated orgasmic session between these men.

When the *real* shit hits the fan, that's when they must decide how far they are able to take this relationship emotionally. You see, both tend to run away. Mr. Sag will literally put on his clothes and slip out the bathroom window. (Oh, hell, let's be honest; he'll just bolt, buck naked.) Pisces men rarely leave, but they know how to be there but not be present (hence the alcohol, drugs, hairspray . . . whatever gets them high and away from the pain).

These men could actually transform themselves and each other if they have the courage to face their demons together. But if one is looking to skip down a destructive path, look out.

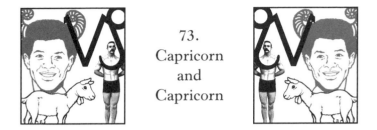

73.
Capricorn
and
Capricorn

Sex and power are linked in our world more than we like to talk about. Between two Capricorn men these loaded issues are irrevocably linked and you can bet they will *never* talk about it. Being earth signs, Capricorn men like to express themselves in tangible ways. Physical love and material gifts are the first things to come to mind, although these Goats do have a reputation for being cheapskates! Together they could bring out the best in each other, teaching and learning together how to be generous. Or they can go to their separate corners and come out only when they want to fight or have sex.

There's definitely a chilly undertone to this relationship. They may not like having their less than lovable characteristics mirrored back at them through the other's behavior. But if these boys can fall in love with their dark sides, they can form a positively transformational union together.

In the beginning they are likely to keep everything pleasant and businesslike. Want to go out for tapas tonight? Want to come over for sex? Have to get up early tomorrow for a big meeting so you want to sleep in your own bed? Fine. But a more emotional connection will creep up, probably when one wants to stay the night, for a few nights in a row. You see, these fellows are creatures of habit, and they do attach easily. Even though it might be more convenient and *practical* (their favorite word) for them to keep this affair "sex only," it could easily develop into something more if they knock boots over half a dozen times.

They do have a lot in common, of course. Sexually, they like it rough, and they get much more cuddly afterward. Sadistic scenes, with a few well-worn props (they're not sex toy addicts, such as Aquarians . . . Capricorns tend to fetishize a few good leather or wooden items and use them again and again and again), are often followed by tender touching and brotherly chat.

Emotionally they are similar in that they are both driven by career ambition and a desire for conventional validation from the world at large. The problem may be that both men may obsess about their work so much that they don't make quality time for each other. A well-placed moon in Cancer in one of them could help the situation a lot. If the lead-up to their relationship is wrought with bad timing, obstacles, and challenges, this actual bodes well for their chances at happiness in the long run. You see, no Capricorn respects anyone or anything that comes to him too easily. Emotional S/M could be the real bond that brings them together and holds them together.

74.
Capricorn
and
Aquarius

Even though Capricorn is an earth sign, and Aquarius is ruled by air, these guys probably have Mercury, Venus, or Mars in the other's Sun sign. That happens a lot with signs that are next to each other in the zodiac. Connections between their "inner" planets are usually what draw them together. Basically, these guys operate in two different worlds. Mr. Capricorn seeks concrete success in the real world. Mr. Aquarius desires freedom on an esoteric and idealistic level.

So what brings them together? Well, the main thing is an obsession with the outside world. Both (especially the Aquarius) may believe they have insight into themselves, but they don't. Mr. Capricorn is obsessed with status and proving himself. Success in the traditional sense is crucial for his happiness. Mr. Aquarius wants to change the world and considers it a personal failure when the world continues to spin in all the same ways that it always has.

As you can probably already see, intimacy is a tough job for these guys. It is possible though. You see, the Capricorn man, although generally undemonstrative and more likely to go to a board meeting in drag than to do any *gushing,* is actually quite expressive through his behavior. He'll show his feelings by doing helpful, practical things for his Aquarius lover. He'll buy him computer software to help him organize his ideas and get his career into high gear. Or he may defend his Aquarian lover's unconventional point of view, in public, if Mr. Aquarius is criticized, even if he totally disagrees with him in private.

The Aquarius will show his love by communicating in words, lots and lots of words. He loves to talk about the experience of falling in love, although he may not always have the real *feelings* to back it up.

Their real feelings may come out in bed, the place where the destiny of this relationship will be decided. Mr. Aquarius loves to experiment and play with his lover's boundaries in bed. Mr. Capricorn loves to use his own force and to have force used on him in bed. These guys' fetishes could completely clash or make for incredible sexual awakenings for both.

If they are compatible sexually, then they need to find a way to make each other happy in other ways. Both of them have basically cool natures and will probably enjoy discussing politics and going out and mixing with groups of people. They can be a real power couple. But for them to really "get it on" emotionally, both are going to have to do a lot of work.

75. Capricorn and Pisces

These two men are naturally compatible. Earth and water blend easily, as do cardinal signs and mutable ones. They are both incredibly subtle, so it is the texture of their relationship that is most important. As a rule, Capricorn men are restrained and cautious, but the loving, compassionate, and generous nature of the Pisces man could make the stodgy Capricorn open up, and open up fast. Of course, once the Capricorn man has been snared, he will see just what a mess his Pisces lover is. Neptune-ruled Fish tend to have a hard time functioning in the real world, and *that* of course is Mr. Capricorn's specialty. He will love to take care of his Pisces man, and in return, he knows, he will receive unconditional love and support. Their relationship resembles a traditional hetero marriage. That's just how sick and codependent these boys are!

Actually, of course, they will both revel in the conventional aspects of their relationship. They take pride in each other's accomplishments, they can go further sexually and emotionally with each other than they could if they were just tricking around, and they really have true affection for each other.

But since life is all about change, the true test of their love will come over time. Can they grow together or will they grow apart? That is the question. The specter that hangs over this relationship can be summed up in a word: *complacency.* Mr. Capricorn tends to be so fixated on his career success that he secretly considers it a waste of his valuable time to "work" on a relationship. Mr. Pisces is so afraid to be alone that he is likely to retreat into his happy fantasy world during the rocky times with his Capricorn lover.

If both are really committed to this relationship, they have got to rise to the occasion and fight for it from time to time. It's unlikely that outside threats (such as flirty boys or annoying in-laws) can cause any real damage to their union. No. The success or failure of their relationship rests solely on their shoulders.

Sex is bound to be glorious, but it is by no means the measure of the relationship. It's simply the icing on the cake. And of course, Mr. Pisces will have to teach Mr. Capricorn to explore other sexual positions besides the old missionary one. With a little luck and a bit of maintenance, these boys could be the Ozzie and Harriet of the modern gay world. Scary! But cute.

76.
Aquarius
and
Aquarius

Aquarian men are dreamers. They believe in making the world a better place, and all their hopes and dreams are tied in to the future. Together, they have a tendency to live in the future, ignore the past, and remain oblivious to the present. And this is not a bad thing. Upon meeting they may feel as if they have met their "other half." Intellectually, they are incredibly well suited. They can stay up all night arguing politics and literally shedding tears over *critical theory*. They are both complete freaks, and they know it. Both have loved and hated themselves throughout life for being so damn "different." When they find each other, they feel validated . . . as if someone else in the world understands them.

Sexually, they can make the earth move. Both are game for anything and prefer to live their lives naked anyway, so their sex life is apt to be a continual source of fulfillment for both. The passion between them is palpable. Although these men are generally accused of being cold and *unemotional*, they can actually bring out real feeling in each other. Miraculous!

Since both men possess such lofty ideals, they may end up moving on in different directions, to fulfill their ideals. You see, they put their ideals before their personal lives, and ironically, it could be their ideals that pull them apart. For this relationship to work, and to last, traditional rules and concepts must be thrown out, and a new guidebook must be written, one that puts freedom at the top of the list. Somehow, having an "out" brings these guys closer together.

Of course, monogamy is the other looming issue when we talk about a relationship between two Aquarius men. Over 90 percent will choose nonmonogamy, I'm sure, as that is their nature. Aquarians are group-oriented and experimental. Hopefully, they will come to an honest decision together about how to handle their extracurricular activities. Of course, some Aquarian couples may decide to have threesomes together instead of tricking on the side. This arrangement could work quite well. And if one of the guys they do together also happens to be an Aquarius, the third man may join them in a relationship for life!

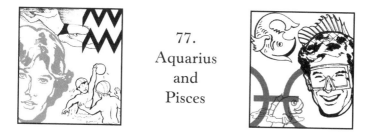

77.
Aquarius
and
Pisces

Both these men are essentially kind and altruistic. Mr. Aquarius, a broad-thinking air sign, wants to release the masses from oppression and help to make the world a better and freer place. Mr. Pisces, a compassionate water sign, wants to heal mankind, one man or woman at a time. Their approaches are different but their motivations are linked.

They may meet while volunteering for a cause they both believe in. Or they may meet while partying on go-go blocks in stiletto heels. These boys both love to feel free and uninhibited, and they love to experiment with substances and with fashion. Their connection is soulful, but oddly distant. You see, the combination of air (Aquarius) and water (Pisces) is a cool one. The Aquarius man seems to understand the world of emotion and imagination that the Pisces man inhabits, but in reality, Mr. Aquarius is more of a thinker and inventor rather than a man who feels and intuits. Naturally, they have a lot to learn from each other, and if the desire is real on both parts, this relationship could be a deep and amazing one.

In their souls, these boys are like two sixties flower children having a love-in. They truly believe "all you need is love" and are likely to fawn all over each other and tell the world about the depth of their feelings, before they even learn each other's middle name and favorite flavor of ice cream. They are both so caught up in the big picture they may forget the little details. Oh, well.

In bed, they will probably both have the feeling of being high (and they very well could be, in the literal sense). Sex has a trippy vibe that both will get off on. They want to alter their minds while making love. And they just may.

When the afterglow fades, it's a real crapshoot as to whether the high will last. The main job for these boys is to get to know each other in a more day-to-day sense. All this talk of love and dreams and dreams and love is great, but what about what your grandparents did for a living and whether you prefer to do your own taxes or hire an accountant? If these boys can remember not to put the cart before the horse, or the "love" before the "like," they will be way ahead of the game.

78.
Pisces
and
Pisces

Pisces men are giving and emotional and could make great partners in life. I suspect, though, that one or both will have to have the strong influence of other signs (ones that are less "floaty" and passive) to make this relationship work. One Pisces tends to feel overly in tune with the mood in the room and in the world and is sometimes immobilized by his fear. Two together may not have the energy and inclination to do anything more than be depressed together or get drunk together (ah, that Piscean tendency toward escaping reality). However, assuming that one has a healthy dose of fire in his chart and the other a good mix of cardinal and fixed signs, this combo could definitely work, and it could be fantastic in a most mystical way.

All Pisces men (especially the gay ones . . . of course!!) are superintuitive, and many of them learn how to develop their latent psychic ability. Not to be too over the top, *but* . . . if two Pisces men are deeply drawn to each other, they are probably feeling the effects of some past-life connections. If they are basically good to each other, chances are they have done right by each other in past incarnations and want to continue their magical love.

The problem with two Pisces men in a relationship is that they may take for granted that they just "know" how the other is feeling and what the other is thinking. In reality, these two space cadets barely understand their own feelings. Ask one Pisces "What did you have for breakfast?" or "How do you feel about your new job?" and the dear boy will probably smile and mutter something adorable and nonsensical. He lives in his own "out there" world. So you can imagine what it's like for two Pisces men to communicate!

Of course, when it comes to making love, that's when it all comes together (and coming together is a favorite activity for them). Who needs to talk? They don't. Except when they are acting out their favorite fantasy scripts, but that's different. Pisces men have a strong connection in spirit, and that may be enough to carry them for a whole lifetime. In fact, two Pisces men from completely different backgrounds and cultures could be great together. Of course, if they can put their thoughts into words, that would make it even easier.

Their greatest characteristics—compassion and imagination—are two wonderful traits that can hold them together. If they're careful around booze and hire a houseboy to translate the day-to-day stuff for them, they will be set for life.